3-03

DISCARD

United States Presidents

George H. W. Bush

Series Consultant:
Don M. Coerver, professor of history
Texas Christian University, Fort Worth, Texas

Michael A. Schuman

Enslow Publishers, Inc.

40 Industrial Road   PO Box 38
Box 398   Aldershot
Berkeley Heights, NJ 07922   Hants GU12 6BP
USA   UK

http://www.enslow.com

To the victims of the terrorist attacks on September 11, 2001, and the heroes who shined that day.

Library of Congress Cataloging-in-Publication Data

Schuman, Michael.
    George H.W. Bush / by Michael A. Schuman.
        p. cm. — (United States presidents)
Summary: Explores the life of the forty-first president, including his service in the Navy, his years in politics, and his impact on United States history.
Includes bibliographical references and index.
    ISBN 0-7660-1702-8
    1. Bush, George, 1924– —Juvenile literature. 2. Presidents—United States—Biography—Juvenile literature. [1. Bush, George, 1924– 2. Presidents.] I. Title. II. Series.
E882 .S34 2002
973.928'092—dc21

                                        2002008158

Printed in the United States of America

10 9 8 7 6 5 4 3 2 1

To Our Readers: We have done our best to make sure all Internet addresses in this book were active and appropriate when we went to press. However, the author and the publisher have no control over and assume no liability for the material available on those Internet sites or on other Web sites they may link to. Any comments or suggestions can be sent by e-mail to comments@enslow.com or to the address on the back cover.

Illustration Credits: Brian Blake, George Bush Presidential Library, p. 99; © Corel Corporation, p. 75; George Bush Presidential Library, pp. 8, 12, 16, 20, 22, 26, 30, 32, 39, 64, 69, 72, 89, 97; Michael A. Schuman, pp. 103, 105; Ronald Reagan Library, p. 58.

Source Document Credits: George Bush Presidential Library, pp. 10, 28, 34, 50, 77, 92.

Cover Illustration: George Bush Presidential Library

Contents

1 Storm in the Desert.   5

2 "Have Half"   9

3 Off the Waters of Chichi Jima. 19

4 Black Gold 29

5 Goodbye Zapata,
   Hello Washington 41

6 Mr. Vice President. 53

7 Campaign '88 63

8 Farewell to the Dictators 71

9 Promises, Promises 81

10 "Not the Position I Would
    Have Preferred" 91

11 Legacy. 101

   Chronology. 107

   Chapter Notes. 111

   Further Reading 121

   Internet Addresses 123

   Places to Visit 125

   Index. 127

1

STORM IN THE DESERT

P resident George Bush never wanted a war. But here it was, February 24, 1991, and American warplanes were dropping bombs half a world away over the ancient city of Baghdad. Baghdad is the capital of Iraq, an oil-rich country in the barren desert of the Middle East.

The conflict started six months earlier, in August 1990, when Iraq invaded its neighbor Kuwait, a much smaller nation also abundant in oil. Iraq had the fourth largest army in the world, and there was no way the little country of Kuwait could successfully fight Iraq on its own.[1]

The Security Council of the United Nations (UN), a group of nations formed in 1945 to promote world peace, told Iraq it must leave Kuwait immediately. President Bush gave Iraq a deadline. If it did not leave Kuwait by January 15, 1991, there would be war. Bush firmly stated that his main concern was the liberation of the Kuwaiti people.

Some Americans questioned Bush's motives. People

5

rely on oil to run their cars, heat their homes, and use anything made from plastic, an oil by-product. These opponents said there was plenty of oil the United States could import from other nations. To them, Bush's real goal was to keep oil flowing to the United States so American oil companies could continue to make money. However, the critics were in the minority. Most Americans supported Bush's tough stand against Iraq.

Iraq's leader, a dictator named Saddam Hussein, would not budge. He claimed that Kuwait was once a province of Iraq, although he never provided concrete proof to back up that statement.

Through skilled diplomacy, Bush was able to form a coalition by getting the support of many other nations, including most Arab countries. That was a major accomplishment, since Arab leaders tend to side with one another.

The January 15 deadline came and was ignored by Iraq. Early in the morning of January 17, 1991, Iraqi time, B-52 bombers flown by American pilots lit up the skies over Baghdad as they dropped cruise missiles on Iraqi military targets. American F-117A Stealth fighters and Navy A-6s added to the massive aerial assault. At the same time, American warships in the Persian Gulf and the Red Sea fired Tomahawk land attack missiles on Iraqi targets. War had begun. Bush named it Operation Desert Storm.

After the first night of fighting, United States pilots had knocked out Iraq's key nuclear and biological sites and its western air defense system. While the Americans had accepted that the allies might lose as many as seventy-five planes, they had lost only two.[2]

The air war continued well into February. Thanks to

artificial satellites beaming television signals across the globe, Americans sitting comfortably in their living rooms watched on television as bombs fell in faraway Iraq. It was the first major war which could be watched live by television viewers from all corners of planet Earth.

On February 24 at four o'clock in the morning in Iraq, the most treacherous part of the war began. This was the ground war, where casualties could be far greater and deaths more grisly than in the air war.

Bush wrote in his diary about Saddam Hussein, "The truth of the matter is that we're going to have to capture his army, and we're going to have to get rid of a lot of that armor. Otherwise, we will have diminished his military, but we will not have accomplished our real goals."[3]

In the thick of the night, American marines and an army tank brigade crossed the border from Saudi Arabia into eastern Kuwait. Behind them were Arab soldiers from Kuwait, Saudi Arabia, Syria, Egypt, and other countries. At the same time, army divisions from the United States, France, and Great Britain invaded western Kuwait and Iraq. By the end of the first day of the ground war, ten thousand weary Iraqi soldiers had surrendered.[4]

As the sun was setting on the ground war's second day, United States Marines had encircled Kuwait's capital, Kuwait City. They were well ahead of their goal. But on that day, Americans realized they could be victims, too. A total of twenty-eight American servicemen and women died when a missile fired by the Iraqis smashed into a barracks.

On February 26, the ground war's third day, Kuwait City was liberated. At the time the fourth day of fighting was ending, the Iraqi military was on the run. Well over half of Iraq's military divisions had been destroyed. Army general Colin Powell was the chairman of the Joint Chiefs of Staff, the president's most trusted group of military advisors. Powell informed Bush, "Mr. President, it's going much better than we expected. The Iraqi army is broken. All they're trying to do now is get out."[5]

Bush declared the fighting was over. Just past 9 o'clock in the evening on February 27, 1991, Bush went on television and addressed the American people. He beamed, "Kuwait is liberated. Iraq's army is defeated. Our military objectives are met. Kuwait is once more in the hands of Kuwaitis, in control of their own destiny."[6]

Army general Colin Powell, shown here leading a meeting with President Bush, was the chairman of the Joint Chiefs of Staff. Powell was one of the president's most trusted military advisors.

2

"HAVE HALF"

United States presidents have come from many backgrounds. Some were raised in poor homes. Abraham Lincoln and Harry Truman fit into that category. Others grew up in unstable families. These would include Bill Clinton and Ronald Reagan. Then, there are those who had the best of all worlds. They were raised in sound, wealthy homes. Examples include Franklin Roosevelt and George Bush.

George Herbert Walker Bush was born June 12, 1924, in Milton, Massachusetts. His father, Prescott Bush, worked for Stedman Products, a company that made rubber floor tiling. Prescott's wife, Dorothy, was a stay-at-home mother. George had an older brother named Prescott, Jr., who was born in 1922. Since his father was nicknamed Pres, the oldest son was called Pressy.

SOURCE DOCUMENT

TOWN OF MILTON
Commonwealth of Massachusetts

I, James G. Mullen, Jr., the undersigned hereby certify, that I hold the Office of Town Clerk of the Town of Milton, County of Norfolk, and Commonwealth of Massachusetts, that the Records of Births, Marriages and Deaths are in my custody and that the following is a true copy from the records, as certified by me.

M R-3

WRITE PLAINLY, WITH UNFADING BLACK INK—THIS IS A PERMANENT RECORD
NO RETURN WITH ERASURES OR ALTERATIONS WILL BE ACCEPTED

The Commonwealth of Massachusetts
OFFICE OF THE SECRETARY
DIVISION OF VITAL STATISTICS

RETURN OF A BIRTH

1 PLACE OF BIRTH

County of NORFOLK _____ (City or town)

City or Town of MILTON. No. 173 Adams _____ St. _____ Ward
(If birth occurred in a hospital or Institution, give its NAME instead of street and number)

2 FULL NAME OF CHILD George Herbert Walker Bush.
(If child is not yet named, make supplemental report, as directed)

3 Sex of Child MALE

4 Twin, triplet or other? (Answer only in event of plural births)

5 Born alive or stillborn

6 Date of birth JUNE 12 1924.
(Month) (Day) (Year)

7 FATHER FULL NAME PRESCOTT SHELDON BUSH.

8 MOTHER PRESENT NAME AND MAIDEN NAME DOROTHY WALKER BUSH.

9 RESIDENCE No. 173 ADAMS St. MILTON, (City or town)

10 RESIDENCE No. 173 ADAMS St. MILTON. (City or town)

11 COLOR OR RACE WHITE **AGE** 29 YEARS

12 COLOR OR RACE WHITE **AGE** 23 YEARS

13 BIRTHPLACE COLUMBUS (City or town) OHIO (State or country)

14 BIRTHPLACE KENNEBUNKPORT, MAINE. (City or town) (State or country)

15 OCCUPATION RUBBER MANUFACTURER

16 OCCUPATION HOUSEWIFE

17 Signature of Attendant at birth Thos. R. Goethals M.D. (Physician, parent or other, etc.)

Address No. 443 BEACON St. BOSTON, MASS. (City or town)

Dated JUNE 13 1924. (Month) (Day) (Year) Did above-named personally attend the birth? YES

18 Received at office of city or town clerk JUN 13 1924 (Month) (Day) (Year)

19 A true copy. Attest: _____ REGISTRAR

George Herbert Walker Bush was born in Milton, Massachusetts, on June 12, 1924. This is his official birth certificate.

Young George first saw the light of day in a Victorian house his parents were renting about ten miles south of Boston. He was named in honor of his grandfather, George Herbert Walker. Since his grandfather was known by the nickname Pop, it was natural that his young namesake was called Poppy.

The family of four did not stay long in Massachusetts. When Poppy was six months old, Prescott Bush, Sr. took a job in New York City as an investment banker. The family bought a home in Greenwich, Connecticut, just across the New York state border. It is common for many New York City businessmen to live in Greenwich and commute to their jobs. When George was two, a girl named Nancy was born into the family.

Prescott Bush, Sr. was a muscular man who stood six foot four and weighed two hundred pounds. He had dark hair and spoke with a deep, booming voice. Pres attended a nearby Episcopal church every Sunday. One time he and his wife were attending a formal dinner when one of the speakers used a swearword. The Bushes were so offended that they immediately went home. The Bush children learned that their parents expected the same behavior from them.

Poppy loved playing with his older brother. Although there were five bedrooms in their Greenwich home, Pressy and Poppy chose to share one. Poppy showed a talent at sports, especially baseball. He was gifted with keen hand-eye coordination, and had a swing that allowed him to make solid contact with the ball.

Off the field, Poppy was a big-hearted and friendly boy. A Bush biographer named Fitzhugh Green said, "They used to call him 'Have Half' when he was a kid because he

Young George Bush lived first in Massachusetts, where he was known by the nickname Poppy.

was so generous with whatever he had in terms of food or clothes or baseball bats or whatever. . . . If he had half a piece of pie left, he'd say, 'Have half of mine.'"[1]

Like many wealthy families, the Bushes owned more than one home. They spent summers in a sprawling ten-bedroom house on the edge of the ocean in Kennebunkport, Maine, about thirty miles across the New Hampshire border. Today Kennebunkport is a resort town drawing thousands of tourists every summer. But in the 1920s it was a small village. The Kennebunkport home had been built by George's great-grandfather and grandfather.

Every July the family would climb into their station wagon and Prescott, Sr. would drive them north to the Maine coast. The Bushes would often stay for weeks at a time, with Prescott returning to his job in New York during the week. Poppy would spend carefree days fishing, swimming, taking to the waters in his grandfather's lobster boat, and playing tennis at a private organization called the River Club.

When he was old enough, Pressy entered first grade at the private Greenwich Country Day School. With Pressy gone during the day, Poppy was horribly lonely. Being away from his brother bothered him so much that Prescott and Dorothy allowed George to enter first grade a year early.

Greenwich Country Day School was for boys only and included grades one through nine. It had a strict dress code. All boys had to wear uniforms consisting of pants called knickers, which had bands around their lower legs, and black sweaters with orange stripes on the left sleeve.

Every morning the boys met for an assembly. The

principal, known as the headmaster, gave out severe punishments for misbehaving. For example, any student who talked out of turn during assembly was forced to spend the rest of the assembly standing on his chair.

The boys learned several subjects, but Latin, history, arithmetic, English, geography, and the arts were emphasized. Away from the classroom, the students were given time to take part in sports such as swimming, hockey, soccer, and baseball.

Meanwhile, the Bush family continued to grow. When George was seven his mother had another son, named Jonathan. However, George always remained closest to Pressy.

Because he began school a year early, George was always among the youngest boys in his class. Bush biographer Herbert S. Parmet believes that is why he never "made much of a mark at the school."[2] However, George was respected as a kind and sensitive boy. On one occasion, the boys in another grade were taking part in an obstacle course race. It was visitors day, when students' parents and other relatives were in attendance. As the race progressed, one overweight boy became stuck in a barrel and began crying. Other students and spectators laughed at the poor boy's expense. George left the spectators' section, stepped onto the field, helped the boy out of the barrel, and ran alongside him for the rest of the race.

In the fall of 1937, when George was thirteen, he left Greenwich to attend a school where he would live on campus, far from home. It was a preparatory school, or prep school, called Phillips Andover Academy. The purpose of a prep school is to help teenagers become ready for college.

Phillips Andover is in the town of Andover,

Massachusetts, about one hundred eighty miles from Greenwich. Like Greenwich Country Day School, all the students at Andover were male. Nearly all were from wealthy families. For a long time, education experts criticized schools such as Andover for not allowing students to be creative or think independently. Still, prep school students were generally respected for being intelligent and hard working.

The motto of Phillips Andover is a Latin term, *Non Sibi*, which means "not for self." Andover boys were taught to be generous and to get along with fellow classmates. Courses were hard and demanded a lot of studying. Difficult tests were given regularly. The boys learned about all kinds of subjects. Arithmetic and the literature and history of ancient Greece and Rome were among the more important ones. Like Greenwich Country Day School, Andover also required its students to learn about the arts and to participate in sports.

Bush was an average student at Andover. One of his English teachers named Hart Day Leavitt remembered having "very little respect for George's mentality."[3] A classmate named Elliott Vose said that Bush was not "one of the brains in the class by a long shot."[4] However, Frank DiClemente, a physical education instructor who also taught biology and chemistry, said Bush did very well in school.

As usual, George proved he was a skilled athlete, excelling in soccer and baseball. He was also popular with the other boys who regarded him as a nice guy who could get along with anyone. One time he witnessed a school bully picking on a younger, smaller boy named Bruce Gelb. The bigger kid ordered Bruce to move a huge couch. Gelb

George (front row, center) proved himself a skilled athlete at Andover, excelling in soccer and baseball.

carried it a small distance before dropping it. He said he could not carry it anymore.

The bully grabbed Bruce's arm and twisted it behind his own back. Bush barked at the bully to leave Gelb alone. The bigger boy walked away. After Bush left, Gelb asked who was the brave kid who rescued him. The boys there replied, "That was Poppy Bush. He's the finest guy in the school. He's a great athlete and everybody loves him."[5]

While away from home at Andover, Bush heard more news from Greenwich. In 1938, his mother gave birth to another son. He was named William, but would be known by the nickname Bucky. He was the last of Bush's siblings.

In his senior year at Andover, Bush noticed a rash on his right arm. Doctors diagnosed it as an infection known as staph, a bacteria officially called staphylococcus. Today, a medicine called sulfanilamide, or sulfa, is used to cure staph.

There was no sulfa medicine in 1941. Bush spent several weeks in a Boston hospital. His older brother Prescott, Jr. said that George was near death for a time while recovering from the infection. He got better, but missed several weeks of classes. Bush stayed an extra year at Andover in order to make up the studies he missed.

Bush's second senior year was his best in school. He captained both the soccer and baseball teams. Because he played fairly, it was hard for others to be jealous. Bush's brother Jonathan said, "He was too big a hero, too big a star. You were just too anxious to get close to him."[6]

In the middle of Bush's final year at Andover, an event halfway across the world took place which would affect the lives of millions of people. On Sunday, December 7, 1941, Japan bombed the United States Naval Base at Pearl Harbor, Hawaii. The next day United States President Franklin Roosevelt asked Congress to declare war against Japan and Congress did so. Shortly afterwards, Germany declared war on the United States. The United States was soon fully involved in World War II.

A few weeks later Bush went home to Greenwich during the Christmas break. While there he attended a dance at the Greenwich Country Club. A pretty brown-haired girl wearing a red and green dress caught his eye. She was Barbara Pierce, the sixteen-year-old daughter of a wealthy magazine publisher. Bush asked a friend to introduce him to her. He did so, and they spent the evening dancing to the popular swing music of the day.

When Christmas vacation was over, Bush returned to school. He also stayed in touch with Barbara by writing letters almost daily. They did not see each other again until spring vacation. Later that year, George took her to his senior prom.

Bush graduated Phillips Andover Academy in June 1942. A few days later, on June 12, he turned eighteen. He was old enough to join the United States armed forces.

3

OFF THE WATERS OF CHICHI JIMA

George Bush said that after the bombing of Pearl Harbor, "There was a surge of patriotism in the whole country and I think I felt that."[1] Like many young men in 1942, he enlisted in the military. Since he had always found the Navy appealing, he chose that branch of service and decided to become a Navy flyer.

On August 6, 1942, Bush said goodbye to his parents and Barbara and boarded a train bound for the naval air station at Chapel Hill, North Carolina. Bush confessed, "It was the first time I had ever seen my dad cry."[2]

The high school graduate's first step was to go through intense training to get into peak physical shape. For the next ten months, Bush was transferred to naval air bases across the country including ones in Minnesota, Texas, and Florida. Then on June 9, 1943, he received his ensign's commission and aviator's wings. It was three days before his nineteenth birthday, making him the youngest Navy flyer in the United States at the time.[3]

Bush was assigned to fly a big, bulky, single-engine torpedo airplane called the Avenger. He spent the middle of the summer of 1943 practicing how to fly and land it. His first drills consisted of landing the plane on a runway measured to be about the same size as an aircraft carrier deck. By late August, he was testing his landings on an actual carrier at sea, the USS *Sable*.

George stayed in touch with his family and Barbara through mail. In a letter he wrote to his mother, George put his feelings about Barbara on paper. He wrote, "I do

As a Navy flyer, Bush flew a single-engine torpedo airplane called the Avenger.

still love (I honestly feel sure of it) Barbara, Mum, yet I know that there is such a chance of her meeting some other guy. She is so very young and so darn attractive and I could hardly expect her to keep caring for me for years. ENOUGH OF THIS!!!!!!!! You both must think I'm crazy!"[4]

In late summer, Bush was given leave, or special permission, to go off duty. He returned to Kennebunkport to be with his family. Barbara joined them and they spent seventeen days sailing, playing tennis, sunbathing on the beach, and attending family gatherings. Bush allowed his eleven-year-old brother Jonathan to hang around. Jonathan remembered those happy days. He said, "George invariably wanted to go sailing, but once we got on the boat he would just stretch out and go on kidding Barbara while I did the actual sailing and Barbara rubbed George's back."[5]

George and Barbara became engaged that summer. At first, they wanted to keep it a secret. They did not know if their families would approve since they were still teenagers. In addition, Bush was going to be fighting in a war. There was always a danger he would not return alive.[6]

In late September, Bush returned to the navy and was transferred with his squadron one more time. Their new home was the Naval Air Station at Chincoteague, Virginia, a narrow peninsula between Chesapeake Bay and the Atlantic Ocean. They spent their days practicing bombing runs. The men flew their Avengers over bombing targets on a nearby field where they dropped fake torpedoes. Sometimes the young pilots had a little fun by flying as close to the land or the surface of the water as possible. They called that "flat-hatting."

One time Bush flat-hatted over a fairgrounds where a

As a pilot, Bush (center) spent his days practicing bombing runs with the rest of his squadron.

traveling circus was setting up. The airplane scared a circus elephant, which charged and frightened people nearby. The mayor lashed out at the base commander, who formally scolded and punished Bush. The other pilots teased Bush good-naturedly by calling him Ellie the Elephant.

In the late fall of 1943, Barbara and George announced their engagement. As they had suspected, their parents were concerned they were too young to be married. But the parents thought the situation over and agreed that the two were sensible, in love, and a good match. The engagement was announced in *The New York Times* on December 12, 1943.[7]

Just three days later, Bush and his crew went to Philadelphia to see an aircraft carrier called the *San Jacinto* be formally commissioned. The men would call it the *San Jac*, and it would be their home for the next several months. On March 25, 1944, the crew boarded the *San Jac* as it left Philadelphia. It sailed through the Panama Canal to San Diego before reaching the Navy base at Pearl Harbor, Hawaii, on April 20. On May 2, it was approved for action. In a matter of days, George Bush and his fellow pilots would be fully involved in the business of war. The *San Jac* soon left Hawaii and headed west towards several islands in the Pacific Ocean being occupied by Japan.

There was a total of sixteen hundred men on the *San Jac*. The new carrier was part of an enormous fleet including fifteen other aircraft carriers and many battleships, cruisers, and supply ships needed to support them. In total, about two hundred thousand men were part of the huge armada.[8]

On May 23, Bush and two other men took off on their first mission in their Avenger, which Bush named "the

Barbara." Their job was to bomb ground installations on Wake Island, which was occupied by Japan. Bush's gunner, Lee Nadeau, remembered, "As we approach the target, naturally the adrenaline starts to flow because you know you're over enemy territory. It wasn't until we had gone down and dropped our bomb load and were pulling away that it registered on me that these guys were shooting at us. It wasn't like practice anymore."[9]

Bush admitted he was scared. "I think everybody I flew with would confess to having a certain amount of fear in their hearts at times and I have never been apologetic about that."[10]

The mission lasted twenty-eight seconds. It was successful. Bush, Nadeau, and the *Barbara's* third crew member, John Delaney, flew many more missions that summer. Not all involved dropping bombs. On several occasions, they flew pre-invasion flights to photograph Japanese positions on islands. The pictures were used to locate gun emplacements or sites where it would be easiest for boats or tanks to land.

On June 19, the *Barbara* was airborne when Bush realized the plane had lost almost all its fuel pressure. He had to make an emergency landing. Since the *San Jac* was not in a position to take the plane, the crew had to land in the water. Nadeau said, "I was scared as hell riding on two thousand pounds of TNT, but Bush made a beautiful landing."[11] Bush exited the plane, went out onto one of its wings, and inflated the life raft, which is mandatory equipment. The men entered the life raft and rowed away from the airplane wreckage.

While on the life raft, Nadeau and Delaney began singing, "Sailing, sailing, over the bounding main."

Nadeau remembered that Bush turned around and said, "You guys had better shut up, or they're going to think we're having too good a time out here."[12] Shortly afterwards, they were rescued by a passing American destroyer. However, the *Barbara* was a total loss and sank into the waters of the Pacific Ocean.

Bush, Nadeau, and Delaney were given another Avenger, which Bush named the *Barbara II*. They flew several more successful missions over the course of the summer of 1944. Then, on September 2, Bush faced what would be the most frightening day of his life.

The crew's assignment was to take out a radio tower being used by the Japanese on an island called Chichi Jima. Bush's partner Lee Nadeau was not on board when the *Barbara II* took off at 7:15 A.M. A lieutenant named Ted White requested to go in his place. He wanted a chance to check out the Avenger's weapons systems. The commander approved.

About an hour after takeoff, the *Barbara II* was hit by Japanese anti-aircraft fire. Bush remembered, "it was as if a massive fist had reached up and crunched the belly of the plane."[13] At 8:40, Bush parachuted out of the plane. In doing so, he hit his head on the plane's tail. When he hit the water, the life raft inflated but Bush had trouble finding it. Blood was gushing out of his head as he floundered in the water, until he finally located the raft and climbed aboard it.

Bush noticed that the raft's paddles had sunk and he had no way to steer the craft. The wind was pushing him towards Chichi Jima. If he landed on shore, he surely would have been taken prisoner by the Japanese. It was

George married Barbara Pierce on January 6, 1945.

learned after the war that some prisoners were eaten by the island's occupiers.

Using all the strength he could muster, Bush paddled with his hands against the wind. Since he had swallowed a lot of seawater, he was nauseous. Every so often he stopped paddling to vomit into the water.

After being afloat for three hours, Bush was located by an American submarine, the *Finback*. The sub's men pulled him on board. Soon afterwards, Bush learned that Delaney and White had died in the attack.

Bush stayed on the *Finback* for eight weeks. He was then permitted to take some leave. He rejected that idea and went where he felt he was needed, back with his men on the *San Jac*.

Late that year, Bush did return home for several weeks. Shortly after 1944 had turned into 1945, he and Barbara Pierce were married on January 6 in Barbara's hometown of Rye, New York.

Bush was honored with the Distinguished Flying Cross, an award for heroism. Yet the war was not over, and his time in the military was not finished. Over the next few months, the young married man was sent to naval bases in Florida, Michigan, Maine, and Virginia to be trained for a major mission; the invasion of the island nation of Japan.

That invasion never happened. The United States dropped two atomic bombs on Japan on August 6 and 9. Japan surrendered and World War II was over.

In total, George Bush had completed 1,228 hours of flying time and took part in 58 missions.[14] He was a true war hero.

SOURCE DOCUMENT

United States Pacific Fleet

Commander Second Carrier Task Force

Pacific Fleet

In the name of the President of the United States, the Commander Second Carrier Task Force, United States Pacific Fleet, presents the DISTINGUISHED FLYING CROSS to

LIEUTENANT (JUNIOR GRADE) GEORGE HERBERT WALKER BUSH
UNITED STATES NAVAL RESERVE

for services as set forth in the following

Citation

"For distinguishing himself by heroism and extraordinary achievement while participating in aerial flights in line of his profession as pilot of a torpedo plane during the attacks by United States Naval forces against Japanese installations in the vicinity of the Bonin Islands on 2 September 1944. He led one section of a four plane division which attacked a radio station. Opposed by intense anti-aircraft fire his plane was hit and set afire as he commenced his dive. In spite of smoke and flames from the fire in his plane he continued in his dive and scored damaging bomb hits on the radio station, before bailing out of his plane. His courage and complete disregard for his own safety, both in pressing home his attack in the face of intense and accurate anti-aircraft fire, and in continuing in his dive on the target after being hit and his plane on fire, were at all times in keeping with the highest traditions of the United States Naval Service."

John S. McCain
Vice Admiral, U. S. Navy

Don Rhodes Box
"Navy 1 of 3"

In 1945, Bush received the Distinguished Flying Cross for heroism.

4

BLACK GOLD

Like many World War II veterans, George Bush made up for lost time by going to college right away. In September 1945, he enrolled as a freshman at Yale University. With so many returning veterans, his class totaled eight thousand incoming students. It was the biggest freshman class in the history of Yale.[1]

At age twenty-one, Bush was three years older than a typical college freshman. Unlike most students, he was a married man. The next year, 1946, he became a father. Barbara gave birth on July 6 to the couple's first child, a son they named George Walker Bush. For those reasons, he was more mature than most college freshman. When younger students were at parties and on dates, Bush had his head buried in books.

All college students must choose a subject to major in. They will take more courses in that subject than any other.

29

Bush's first son, George Walker Bush, was born on July 6, 1946.

Bush chose economics. He had his eye on a business career after he graduated. Bush was a better student at Yale than he had been at Andover. He earned membership in Phi Beta Kappa, an honors society which only the most excellent college students can join. He also was accepted into an exclusive Yale club called Skull and Bones. In addition, he found time to head a fund-raising drive for the United Negro College Fund, an organization which helps poor African-American students pay for college educations.

If that was not enough, Bush played on Yale's varsity soccer and baseball teams. He excelled at both sports, but liked baseball better. A first baseman, Bush was chosen to be the team captain in his senior year. There was so much talent on the squad that five players were drafted by major league teams.

Yale made it to the College World Series that year against the University of Southern California. In a best of three series, Yale lost two games to one. Perhaps the highlight of Bush's baseball experiences did not take place during a game. Baseball legend Babe Ruth honored Yale by donating the original copy of his autobiography to the university library. As captain, Bush accepted the manuscript from the celebrated Ruth in a formal ceremony. Just a few months later, Ruth died from throat cancer.

Bush graduated Yale in three years instead of the usual four. It is thought that major league scouts were ready to make Bush an offer to play professional baseball. His offensive statistics were weak. In fifty-one games, he hit only .251, with two home runs and twenty-three runs batted in. He shined at first base, though, making 442 outs, handling 24 assists, and committing just 9 errors.[2]

But Bush's career was headed in another direction: the oil fields of west Texas. The young graduate could have easily taken a job working for his father's investment firm, but George refused. There were many opportunities in the oil industry for hard-working risk takers. Bush wrote to a friend named Gerry Bemiss, "Fortunes can be made in the land end of the oil business, and of course can be lost."[3] Bush was willing to take that chance. After all, so many had had success in the business that oil was referred to as black gold.

However, he did take advantage of his family's influence to embark on his new career. Prescott Bush was an officer in Dresser Industries, a huge oil supply

While Bush was at Yale, baseball great Babe Ruth donated the original copy of his autobiography to the university. Bush accepted the book in a formal ceremony.

company. A family friend, Neil Mallon, was Dresser Industries president. Mallon offered George a job as a trainee equipment clerk, and he accepted. Just two months after graduating college, Bush drove to Odessa, Texas, by himself in a 1947 Studebaker Champion, a graduation gift from his parents. After he found a place to live, Barbara moved out west with their baby.

Odessa is three hundred fifty miles west of Dallas in eastern Texas and three hundred miles east of El Paso in extreme western Texas. It sits near its twin city of Midland in the heart of the Texas plains, where the sun boils the land in summer. Some Texans regard it as in the middle of nowhere. Many Odessa residents were rowdy oil field workers who lived in houses not much bigger that shacks. It was totally different from the comfortable world Bush had grown up in.

Why did Bush decide to move so far from home into such a different setting? There was of course the business opportunity. In addition, Bush wanted to step out from under the shadow of his father. He wanted to show he could succeed on his own. He wrote, "We were young, still in our early twenties, and we wanted to make our way, our own mistakes, and shape our own future."[4]

Despite his background and education, Bush started his new life from the ground up. His first jobs included cleaning and painting oil equipment. Within a year he moved up to the position of assemblyman for a division, or separate part, of Dresser Industries, called Pacific Pumps. This meant a move to southern California.

The Bushes took up residence in Huntington Park, outside Los Angeles. More moves were in order. Bush became a salesman, and within roughly a year lived in the

SOURCE DOCUMENT

That's where the white-collar workers lived. The blue-collar workers, like us, lived in Odessa. A week after his arrival, George finally called to say that he had found a tiny place and we should come down. He said it was a sorry little house, and it was. But Georgie and I were so excited about being with him. This was an adventure the three of us had signed up for together.

We stepped off the plane—a 12-hour flight in those days—to a whole new and very hot world. Odessa is flat as a pancake and as different to Rye, N.Y., as any place you've been. Nothing comes easy to West Texas. Every tree must be cultivated, and every flower is a joy.

As far as my mother was concerned, we could have been living in Russia. Who ever heard of Odessa, Texas? She sent me cold cream, soap and other items she assumed were only available in civilized parts of the country. She did not put Odessa in that category. I loved getting all that stuff free, but eventually had to write and tell her we had big, beautiful super markets—which Rye did not have at the time.

Barbara Bush wrote this description of her arrival in Odessa, Texas, and what life was like there for the Bushes.

California cities of Bakersfield, Ventura, and Compton. He spent his days driving to and from oil businesses, trying to convince them to buy his company's drill parts. It was in Compton in 1949 that the Bushes had their second child, a daughter named Pauline Robinson Bush. Called Robin for short, she had blonde hair and blue eyes and was a very happy baby.

Bush was doing so well with sales that, in April 1950, Dresser Industries called him back to Texas. He was given a better paying sales job and was headquartered in Midland. Although Midland is just twenty miles from Bush's former home in Odessa, it is a very different city. While most people in Odessa worked in the actual oil fields, most Midland residents spent their days in the oil companies' offices as sales people, clerks, and managers. Many were educated people from the East, just like the Bushes.

After three and a half years with Dresser Industries, Bush began growing restless. In the spring of 1951, he decided to start his own business. He was concerned what his friend and mentor Neil Mallon would say about him leaving.[5] To Bush's delight, Mallon responded, "I really hate to see you go, George, but if I were your age, I'd be doing the same thing. And here's how I'd go about it."[6] Mallon then gave his salesman free advice on how to run a company.

Bush joined forces with his next door neighbor, John Overbey, to form the Bush-Overbey Oil Development Company, Inc. The business consisted mainly of buying what are called oil royalty rights from small landowners and selling them to bigger oil companies. A royalty is the share of a profit.

Back home in Connecticut, there was some big news. Bush's father, Prescott Bush, was elected to the United States Senate in 1952 to complete the term of a senator who had died in office. He ran as a moderate to liberal Republican and won in a heavily Democratic state by thirty thousand votes.[7] That same election campaign, George worked locally for General Dwight D. Eisenhower for president. Eisenhower, a World War II hero, was the Republican nominee. Republicans were thrilled when Eisenhower was elected, ending twenty years of Democratic rule in the White House.

There was exciting news in Midland, too. In February 1953, another Bush child was born. It was a boy named John Ellis Bush. Because his initials spelled out "JEB," that became his nickname.

Life was going well for the Bushes until one day they received the worst news any parents could hear. Robin, then four years old, had been acting very tired and listless. She was taken to a doctor and was diagnosed with a form of blood cancer known as leukemia. Although a doctor in Midland said Robin's disease was incurable, the Bushes refused to give up hope. They took her to New York City to Memorial Sloan-Kettering Hospital, one of the country's best cancer treatment centers.

However, the cancer was deadly. Robin died in October 1953. George and Barbara grieved for months. Barbara wrote, "We awakened night after night in great physical pain—it hurt that much."[8]

The Bushes never got over Robin's death, but life went on. They felt very much at home in Midland. When not hosting neighborhood barbecues on their small patio, George coached Little League baseball where he impressed the townspeople with his talents. Both Bushes taught Sunday school at the First Presbyterian Church and volunteered at the local YMCA and in regional theater groups.

Barbara once complained that when her husband got together with friends, all they did was discuss business. They had good reason to. Bush-Overbey was making much money, and attracted the attention of two Midland brothers, William and Hugh Liedtke. In 1953, the Liedtkes suggested that Bush and Overbey join them in a new oil investment company. They agreed, and a deal was reached.

The new business needed a name. A popular movie showing at a Midland theater at the time was called *Viva Zapata!* starring Marlon Brando. It was a biography of a noted Mexican revolutionary. Since the name was famous at that moment, the four men decided to take advantage and call their business Zapata Petroleum.

The nation's economy was growing steadily in the decade after World War II ended. Americans were feeling good about their country, but there was also much fear. It stemmed from a huge dispute with what was then the second major superpower on the planet: the Soviet Union. Because no actual fighting ever took place, this conflict was known as the Cold War.

The hostility had its roots in the two countries' differences in government. The United States is a democratic capitalist country. That means that all businesses are owned by private persons or companies.

The Soviet Union, the other major world power at the time, was a Communist country. In pure Communism, all businesses are owned by the community (all the citizens of a country). There is no private business. In the Soviet

Union, all businesses were owned by the government. The only official political party was the Communist party. There was no tolerance for people with differing views. Citizens who openly criticized their government were punished. Several countries of eastern Europe were also under communist rule, and their leaders were heavily influenced by the Soviet Union. Many Americans were scared that the Soviet Union was going to force its way of life on the United States.

Some people exploited that fear for their own gain. One who did was a Republican senator from Wisconsin named Joseph McCarthy. He claimed he had lists of names of Communist party members who worked for the United States government. McCarthy never provided any proof, but by making these claims he brought a great deal of attention to himself.

Few people had the courage to publicly challenge McCarthy. Even President Eisenhower, who privately condemned McCarthy, would not take him on in public. One person brave enough to do so was Connecticut Senator Prescott Bush. He turned down a campaign contribution McCarthy offered him and refused to attend a Republican dinner in Connecticut where McCarthy was scheduled to be.

In his private life, Senator Bush was becoming a grandfather many times over as George and Barbara continued adding to their family. In 1955, Barbara gave birth to another son. He was named Neil Mallon Bush, in honor of their family friend. The next year, she had another son, called Marvin Pierce Bush after her father.

As the family grew, so did Zapata Petroleum. In the mid-1950s, Bush decided to give his attention to offshore

The Bush family continued to grow. In 1955, Barbara gave birth to Neil Mallon Bush, and in 1956, Marvin Pierce Bush was born.

oil drilling. The term "offshore" refers to oil supplies under water. While the Liedtkes concentrated on land drilling, Bush set his sights on the waters off the Texas coast near Galveston, nearly six hundred miles southeast of Midland. The Liedtkes, Overbey, and Bush decided that they should form a company division in charge only of the offshore drilling business. It was called Zapata Off-Shore, and Bush was named its president.

In 1956, Bush again worked on a local level for Eisenhower as the president ran for a second term. Eisenhower was reelected in a landslide. While Bush was thrilled with the election result, his heart was in his job.

Over the next several years, the two Zapata businesses began to grow more separate. The Liedtke brothers were directly involved in exploring for oil. Bush, meanwhile, was renting drilling equipment to other companies who wanted to dig for oil on their own. In 1959, the two companies formally split. With Bush so involved in offshore drilling, it made sense that he move closer to the ocean.

Barbara was upset by the news. She wrote, "I loved Midland and our friends and did not want to leave that cocoon of warmth and love."[9]

The Bushes moved across the state to Houston in the summer of 1959, while Barbara was pregnant with her sixth child. On August 18, 1959, Barbara gave birth to their second daughter, Dorothy Walker Bush. George and the children moved into their new house in Houston while Barbara was in the hospital. This was the beginning of a new life for the Bush family, in more ways than one.

5

GOODBYE ZAPATA, HELLO WASHINGTON

S oon after Bush settled in Houston, local Republicans began to consider him a candidate for public office. He was a war hero, a graduate from one of the nation's best colleges, a volunteer with many community activities, and a devoted husband and father.

Some friends felt Bush would be better off running as a Democrat. Around the time of the Civil War, the Democratic party was the party of states' rights. Southern states believed strongly in states' rights, so the Democrats became the party of the South. One hundred years later that was still true. Up to the 1960s, there was a saying that in Texas, there are two political parties: liberal Democrats and conservative Democrats.

Bush insisted that he was a Republican, since he believed in Republican ideals. One major difference between the parties is that Republicans believe volunteers and private business can best meet people's needs. Democrats generally feel that government programs are best at those requirements, since they say volunteers and private companies cannot be counted on to regularly help poor and needy people. To Republicans, these programs are seen as a burden on the government. Republicans also insist that such programs condition people to rely on others rather than work hard on their own.

Bush noticed that in the early 1960s, Republicans were beginning to make some headway in Texas. The civil rights movement was in full swing. African Americans in the South were tired of living under legal segregation, or separation of the races. Yet to many white Texans, segregation was their way of life. It bothered them that the United States Supreme Court was striking down segregation laws. By now, the Democrats were supporting a strong federal government and Republicans were carrying the banner of state's rights. Southerners were starting to lean towards Republican candidates.

Meanwhile, the Cold War was as strong as ever. In 1961, Communists built what became the most enduring symbol of the Cold War. After World War II, the former German capital of Berlin was divided into east and west sectors. East Berlin was Communist and West Berlin was free. As a result, many people living in East Berlin fled illegally to West Berlin. So many did, that in 1961 the East Berlin government did something drastic. They built a wall separating the two sections to keep East Berlin residents from leaving. Husbands were separated from wives; siblings were separated from siblings. People living in the United States and other democratic countries viewed the wall as a disgraceful symbol of Communism.

With these events dominating the world's news, Bush took his first political job in 1962. He joined the Republican Candidates Selection Committee in Harris County, in Houston. His job there was to help decide who would be top candidates for local political offices. Harris County Republicans soon realized that one of the best was working right alongside them: George Bush.

They urged Bush to run for Senate in 1964, and Bush accepted. He won the state Republican primary in a landslide. Bush would then run in the general election against the popular sitting senator, Democrat Ralph Yarborough.

Yarborough, however, would not be Bush's only opponent. A small but powerful group of extreme anti-Communists called the John Birch Society was attempting to control the Texas Republican party. The John Birch Society believed that the United Nations was controlled by Communists. They even accused President Eisenhower, a five-star general and moderate Republican, of being a tool of the Communists. Many made fun of the John Birch Society for their views, but society members took themselves very seriously.

Mainstream Republicans did not want the John Birch Society to rule their party. So Bush had to distance himself from the group. At the same time, he did not want to appear too liberal. He came out publicly against the 1964 Civil Rights Act, which banned several forms of discrimination against people on the basis of one's race. This was despite the fact that his father had been a strong supporter of the civil rights movement, and that George Bush himself had worked for the American Negro College Fund.

Bush tried to perform a careful balancing act. In doing so, he seemed to anger both sides and satisfy neither. In the end, Yarborough won 57 percent of the vote. Still, Bush's 43 percent was the best a Republican Senate candidate had done in Texas up to that time.[1] It was an especially amazing feat considering that the Democrats won large majorities in both the United States Senate and House of Representatives and Democrat Lyndon Johnson was elected president in a landslide. After the election, Bush confessed to his Episcopalian minister, John Stevens, "You know, John, I took some of the far right positions to get elected. I hope I never do it again. I regret it."[2]

Bush changed his strategy and decided to run for the House of Representatives in 1966. In order to devote full time to politics, he sold Zapata Offshore. This time Bush stayed true to himself while campaigning. He supported civil rights, and took moderate stances on other issues. And this time he won, beating a Democrat named Frank Briscoe, who some voters believed was more conservative than Bush. George Bush was the first Republican congressman ever elected from Harris County.[3]

In Congress, Bush voted mostly along party lines. He was in favor of less government spending and more local government control. On some issues, like the environment, he was a moderate. He even served as chairman of the Republican Task Force on Earth Resources and Pollution. More importantly, Bush was the first freshman congressman to earn a place on the House Ways and Means Committee. That is a very powerful committee in charge of finding methods of increasing government revenue.

At this time, the Vietnam War was raging. North Vietnam, which was Communist, was at war with non-Communist South Vietnam, an ally of the United States.

The United States was actively involved, with its soldiers fighting alongside the South Vietnamese. Some American soldiers voluntarily enlisted to fight in the war, but many more were drafted. That meant they were called on by the government to serve in the military whether or not they wanted to.

At first, the vast majority of Americans supported the war. As years went by, many began having second thoughts. Bush was one who began to question whether the war was worth the lives of American soldiers. He also wondered whether it was winnable. In time Bush supported dropping the draft in favor of an all-volunteer army and a slow but steady withdrawal of United States troops.

Perhaps Bush's boldest step while in Congress was supporting the Fair Housing Act of 1968. It banned selling or renting homes on the basis of race, religion, national origin, and gender. Bush supported the bill, much to the dismay of many Houston residents he represented.

A public meeting was held in Houston to discuss the issue. The audience was filled with angry voters. Bush spoke about minority soldiers risking their lives in Vietnam. He stated, "A man should not have a door slammed in his face because he is a Negro ["Negro" was an accepted term for an African American then] or speaks with a Latin American accent."[4] When he finished speaking, the room erupted in applause.

Some critics have stated that Bush said those words not because he believed them, but for selfish political reasons. Bush had hopes of running for Senate again in 1970. To win that election, Bush would have to win Texas's large Hispanic vote. Critics say he wanted to go on record supporting the bill.

On the other hand, by supporting the bill, Bush might have lost reelection to the House of Representatives. That would have severely hurt his chances of election to the Senate two years later. *The New York Times* later praised Bush, saying that, "It took courage to cast that vote."[5]

Richard Nixon won the Republican nomination for president in the summer of 1968. He considered Bush as a possible running mate, but rejected him as too young. At home, no Democrat challenged Bush for reelection to the House, and he began his second term in January 1969.

Indeed, Bush was looking ahead to the Senate race of 1970. Ralph Yarborough, who had beaten Bush in 1964, planned to run again. However, many Texans had lost confidence in Yarborough, viewing him as too liberal for their state. There seemed to be a strong chance that Bush could beat Yarborough in 1970.

Bush's hopes were dealt a sharp blow. Yarborough lost his party's nomination in the state Democratic primary. A businessman and World War II medal winner named Lloyd Bentsen was chosen as the nominee. His views were more moderate than Yarborough's. In fact, his opinions were similar to Bush's. Bentsen had one huge advantage, though. He was a Democrat in a state which still had a Democratic majority.

Bush's father was one of many who warned the congressman about running against Bentsen. He was risking his seat in the House of Representatives, which appeared a sure thing. On the other hand, President Nixon felt Bush would make a fine senator and urged him to run. The president went so far as to offer Bush a government job if he lost the election.[6] Bush disregarded his father's advice and ran, only to lose to Bentsen. The Democratic winner received about 150,000 more votes than Bush, or about 53 percent of the vote.[7]

Nixon kept his promise and offered Bush an important position: United States ambassador to the United Nations. Bush gladly accepted. His major test at the UN concerned the far off but important country of the People's Republic of China, known among Americans as Communist China. At the time, Communist China was not a member of the UN. The little island of Taiwan, also part of China but a separate non-Communist nation, did belong.

The communist Soviet Union was a strong presence in the UN. In addition, many emerging nations in Africa had been colonies of western European democracies. Now that they were independent, they rejected the countries that had ruled over them for decades and aligned themselves with the Communist nations. This group of nations is generally referred to as the Third World.

The huge voting bloc of the Communist and Third World countries strongly supported the entrance of the People's Republic of China into the UN. However, the leaders of Communist China insisted that they were the only China, as if Taiwan did not exist.

The United States wanted both Chinas represented in the UN. Bush tried hard to convince undecided members to see his point of view. But the final vote to admit Communist China and evict Taiwan was fifty-nine nations for, fifty-five against, and fifteen abstaining, or not voting.[8] Bush was especially disappointed in several countries which said they would vote with the United States but went back on their words. He wrote, "I felt it was a dark moment for the United Nations and international diplomacy."[9]

The summer and fall of 1972 was a difficult time for Bush and the country. It was an election year and President Nixon was running for a second term. In June a handful of men were caught breaking into the Democratic National Headquarters at the Watergate, a building in Washington, D.C. It was soon learned that these men were members of the Committee to Reelect the President (CRP). No one knew then that it would blow up into a major scandal.

Then, in September, a tragedy occurred in an unlikely setting. The Olympics are meant to be a place for people of all nations to compete fairly in sports in a spirit of brotherhood. At the Summer Olympics in Munich, Germany, that year, a group of Arab terrorists sneaked into the Olympic compound and kidnapped and murdered eleven Israeli athletes. In response, Israel bombed bases in Syria and Lebanon where terrorists were being trained. In a formal statement, the UN Security Council condemned Israel for the raid, but not the Arabs who murdered the athletes.

Americans in general had always supported the UN, especially its humanitarian work. However, this vote was perceived by many Americans as proof that the UN had become a prejudiced, anti-democratic organization. Bush said, "It was a one-sided, irresponsible resolution."[10]

Later that month, Prescott Bush, Sr., entered a hospital to undergo surgery for lung cancer. Less than a month later, on October 8, he was dead. His son George poured his heart out in a letter to one of his best friends, C. Fred Chambers, "I guess you, probably more than any of our friends, knew what he meant to me in terms of inspiration in my own life. Wherever I was, whatever I did, he was the incentive behind everything."[11]

In spite of the loss, Bush continued with his work. In fact, over the next four years he held three additional varied but important positions. In January 1973, Bush was named chairman of the Republican National Committee. It was a tough time to be head of his party. There were constant news reports connecting President Nixon to illegal or illicit actions connected to the Watergate scandal.

At first Bush defended Nixon. Then, on August 5, 1974, an audio tape Nixon had secretly made in 1972 became public. On the tape, Nixon appeared to be ordering a cover-up of the investigation into the original burglary. Bush now became one of many Republicans urging the president to resign. Nixon did so on August 8, and Vice President Gerald Ford was sworn in as president.

Ford immediately offered Bush other positions, such as an ambassadorship to a country in Europe. Bush had another nation in mind: the People's Republic of China. The United States did not have diplomatic relations with Communist China, so Bush was not called an ambassador. Instead, his title was "liaison officer." Even though Bush had been angered by the manner in which China was admitted to the UN, he realized how important the Asian nation was to the future of the United States.

The Bushes left for Peking (now Beijing), the capital of China, on October 17, 1974. China was a very closed country, but the Bushes were warmly welcomed. George and Barbara brought their dog, a cocker spaniel they had named C. Fred after Bush's friend, C. Fred Chambers. The citizens of Beijing were delighted at the sight of Bush walking his dog, something rarely seen in China. Since few

August 7, 1974

The Honorable Richard M. Nixon
President of the United States
The White House
Washington, D. C.

Dear Mr. President:

It is my considered judgment that you should now resign. I expect
in your lonely embattled position this would seem to you as an act of
disloyalty from one you have supported and helped in so many ways.

My own view is that I would now ill serve a President, whose
massive accomplishments I will always respect and whose family I
love, if I did not now give you my judgment.

Until this moment resignation has been no answer at all, but given
the impact of the latest development, and it will be a lasting one, I
now firmly feel resignation is best for this country, best for this
President. I believe this view is held by most Republican leaders
across the country.

This letter is made much more difficult because of the gratitude
I will always have for you.

If you do leave office history will properly record your achieve-
ments with a lasting respect.

Very sincerely,

George Bush

*Though he supported Nixon at first, on August 7, 1974, Bush sent
the president a letter urging him to resign.*

own cars in China, Bush and his wife rode bicycles like the residents. Even Bush's seventy-three-year-old mother moved about on a bicycle through the busy streets.

Bush stayed in China only thirteen months, when President Ford called him home to take another position. In January 1976, Bush became director of the Central Intelligence Agency (CIA), a government agency whose job it is to gather information about nations or groups which may be a threat to the United States. Bush's work was so secret that he could not even discuss his day's activities with Barbara.

The CIA had been under attack for involvement in the Watergate scandal and other misuses of power. Bush's job was to help reorganize the CIA to make sure such problems did not occur again. However, in November 1976, Gerald Ford lost the presidential election to Jimmy Carter. A Democrat, Carter wanted to put fellow Democrats in important positions. Bush was let go and returned to Houston, Texas, as a private citizen.

6

MR. VICE PRESIDENT

G eorge Bush moved back to Houston, unemployed for the first time since 1948. But important businesses were eager to have a person with his experience on their staffs.

The former congressman took an executive management job at the First International Bank of Houston. Other companies recruited him, too, and Bush served as a consultant to several. However, Bush wanted to return to public service. Not willing to settle this time for the House of Representatives or the Senate, his goal was the highest position in his country: president of the United States. On May 1, 1979, he formally announced that he was a candidate for the job.

Things looked promising for the Republicans in the upcoming election of 1980. The American economy under President Carter was weak. There were energy shortages with motorists waiting in gas station lines over an hour long to fill up their cars. Then, in November 1979, a strange event occurred in the Middle Eastern country of Iran, which fatally damaged Carter's chances of being reelected.

The mostly Moslem country had been governed by a ruler called a Shah, the equivalent of a king. Many Iranians felt the Shah was unfair to his people. A revolution followed and a fundamentalist Moslem religious leader named Ayatollah Khomeni became Iran's leader. For decades the United States had enjoyed friendly relations with the Shah. In 1979, the United States government even allowed the Shah to enter their country for medical treatment. In response, the citizens of Iran became strongly anti-American. Some extreme Iranian Moslems referred to the United States as the Great Satan.

On November 4, 1979, five hundred Iranians invaded the American embassy in Iran and held ninety Americans as hostages. They threatened to kill them if the United States did not return the Shah to Iran. These kidnappers were fully supported by the Ayatollah Khomeni and the Iranian government.

The United States had never dealt with this type of warfare. They soon realized there was little they could do to get the hostages released safely. The United States had all sorts of powerful weapons, but using them on the Iranian kidnappers would have also killed the hostages. The United States was a helpless giant, and Americans were embarrassed and angry about it. The easiest target for their anger was sitting president Jimmy Carter. Many Americans thought that the Iranians must have seen Carter as a feeble president in order to try to get away with a vicious act such as taking innocent hostages. The American people began to cry out for a strong leader.

After a while, the Iranians released most of the women and African-American hostages, but continued to hold the white males. The hostage total for most of the crisis held at fifty-two.

Republicans were enthusiastic about the chance to take back the White House in the upcoming election. But who would their nominee be? At first there were seven Republicans trying to get the party's nomination for president. The best known was former California Governor Ronald Reagan. He had run for the Republican nomination in 1976 and almost beat sitting President Gerald Ford.

Reagan was a strong conservative, and that bothered some moderate Republicans. He had vigorously supported the Vietnam War, and had harshly criticized war protestors. Critics feared he would take the United States into an unneeded war. Reagan was also sixty-eight years old. His advanced age was also a concern.

The first event of the presidential primary season, the Iowa Caucus, took place January 21, 1980. The caucus is a meeting where members of each party gather and verbally declare who they support for their party's nomination. In a major upset, George Bush beat Reagan and the other Republican candidates. The next day, NBC political correspondent Tom Pettit announced, "I would like to suggest that Ronald Reagan is politically dead."[1]

The next test was the first state primary election, held in New Hampshire on February 25. Unlike the Iowa caucus, this event was a traditional election with secret ballots. Bush claimed he had momentum going into New Hampshire. Reagan campaigned on cutting taxes, spending more money on the military, and at the same time balancing the budget. Bush said there was no way that could be done. He said it would result in a huge deficit, which means the country would be spending more money than it was taking in. He ridiculed Reagan's plan, calling it "voodoo economics." Things were looking bright for Bush. Then, on February 23, came a disaster.

A debate between Reagan and Bush, the two front runners, was scheduled that day in the city of Nashua, New Hampshire. Reagan's staff paid the $3,500 cost of the debate. As the debate was about to start, mass confusion broke out. The other five Republican candidates showed up, all hoping to take part. Reagan suggested the rule be changed to allow all seven candidates in the debate. Bush wanted to limit the debate to himself and Reagan. As Reagan began to speak, debate moderator Jon Breen ordered Reagan's microphone cut off. Reagan snapped loudly, "I paid for this microphone, Mr. Green."[2]

Though Reagan had gotten the moderator's name wrong, he scored a major victory. The audience burst into applause. Reagan looked strong, forceful, and fair-minded. Bush stared at the audience in silence. A New Hampshire newspaper publisher said Bush looked as out of place as a child at the wrong birthday party.

The momentum had switched. Republicans in New Hampshire overwhelmingly voted for Reagan on primary day. The debate calamity may not have been the only reason for their decision, but it did a great deal to hurt Bush's image. People started calling him a name which would haunt him for the rest of his career: wimp.

Although Bush won a few more primaries, Reagan easily earned his party's nomination. The only surprise was who he would pick as a running mate. Reagan would make that announcement at the Republican National Convention that summer in Detroit. Reagan's first choice was an unusual one, former President Gerald Ford. At the convention, Reagan and Ford seriously discussed the matter before Ford turned it down.

Bush and Reagan made amends in Detroit and Reagan selected Bush to be his running mate. Some Republican conservatives were upset that Reagan chose the more moderate Bush, but he was overwhelmingly accepted. The Reagan-Bush ticket easily beat President Jimmy Carter and Vice President Walter Mondale in November.

Although Carter was voted out of office, he and his staff continued to work hard to free the hostages held in Iran. As Carter's term was winding down to its last minutes, an agreement was reached with the Iranian government. The hostages would be set free.

At twelve noon on January 20, 1981, Reagan and Bush were sworn in as president and vice president. Just minutes later, the Iranians released all the American hostages. They seemed to add a final insult to Carter's presidency by freeing the hostages while he was no longer in office.

As vice president, Bush kept to himself any differences of opinion with Reagan. Then, just over two months after taking office, Bush found himself at the center of a crisis. He was in Texas when he received word that President Reagan had been shot after giving a speech in Washington.

Bush rushed back to Washington. After arriving, he refused to take a helicopter to land on the White House south lawn. He said only the president can do that, and he did not want to appear anxious to grab power.

The vice president arrived instead by limousine. While

In 1980, Ronald Reagan became president, with George Bush as his vice president.

in the White House, Bush arranged for an emergency meeting with Reagan's Cabinet. He was careful to sit in his seat and not the president's. He reassured the nation that the government would continue to function smoothly. Reagan eventually recovered, and Bush had proven he could handle an emergency situation.

Vice President Bush was put in charge of a number of task forces, or groups organized to meet specific goals. One tackled the large amounts of illegal drugs being smuggled into south Florida. While more drugs were being captured in the United States than in previous years, it was also true that smugglers were bringing more drugs across the borders than before. Whether the task force succeeded in its mission is open to debate.

A second task force studied ways to combat terrorism, such as the Iranian kidnappings. Its conclusion was, "The United States Government will make no concessions to terrorists."[3] To do so, it reasoned, would encourage more terrorism.

Within a couple of years, the economy began improving. Reagan's supporters took the credit, but critics said the president had little to do with the better times. Some credited Jimmy Carter's conservation policies, which they said led to an oil surplus.

In foreign affairs, Reagan talked tough against both the Soviet Union and Islamic terrorists. Still, extremist Moslems in the war-torn Middle Eastern country of Lebanon continued the practice of kidnapping Americans and holding them as hostages. There was only a handful at any given time, not the huge number that the Iranians had captured. Also, they were not held by a large, organized group like the Iranian students, but by small, secretive bands of fanatics. Reagan's opponents were highly critical, saying that Reagan talked tough but was unable to do anything to free these hostages. In response, Reagan replied that unlike the Iranian students, it was impossible to pinpoint who was responsible for these kidnappings.

Reagan and Bush ran for reelection in 1984. The Democrats nominated former Vice President Walter Mondale as president. For his running mate, Mondale made history by choosing Congresswoman Geraldine Ferraro from New York. She was the first woman in United States history selected as candidate for vice president on a major ticket.

During a debate with Ferraro, Bush blindly supported Reagan's policies. Some observers again called him a wimp, saying he was unable to think for himself. Bush supporters said people confused being a wimp with being loyal. It did not matter since the Reagan-Bush team clobbered Mondale and Ferraro at the polls. Reagan won forty-nine states. Mondale carried only his home state of Minnesota and Washington, D.C.[4]

Through much of his second term, Reagan was frustrated by his inability to free the remaining hostages in Lebanon. As soon as their captors freed one, another would be taken and held. It was suspected that these Islamic extremists had connections to Iran, but little more was known. The United States was desperate to bring the hostages home. In 1986, this desperation erupted into a major scandal.

It was learned that Robert McFarlane, Reagan's national security advisor, had approached Iranian leaders with a deal in mind. Iran was in a prolonged war with its neighbor, Iraq, and needed weapons. The United States wanted the hostages released. Perhaps a trade could be arranged. If the United States secretly sold missiles to Iran to use against Iraq, perhaps Iran would use its influence to free the remaining hostages. Of course, by doing so, the Reagan administration would be breaking its promise about not making concessions to terrorists.

At the same time, there was a civil war taking place in the Central American nation of Nicaragua. A Communist-controlled government was in power. A group of rebels called the Contras was fighting them. President Reagan whole-heartedly supported the Contras. But Congress had passed a law making it illegal for the United States government to give them military aid aimed at overthrowing the government of Nicaragua.

Members of the Reagan administration came up with a way around that problem. They would use some of the money they earned from weapons sales to Iran to fund the Contras in Nicaragua, even though it was illegal. Army officer, Colonel Oliver North, who served under McFarlane, was put in charge of this mission. The affair became known as the Iran-Contra scandal.

Just who was involved in these decisions? That has never been fully learned. McFarlane said that Reagan gave the go-ahead to sell missiles to Iran. Oliver North testified under oath, "I believe that the president had indeed authorized such activity."[5]

Reagan responded by saying he never gave permission to sell the missiles to Iran, nor did he have anything to do with illegally funding the Contras. Was he to be believed? And was Vice President George Bush involved? Secretary of State George Shultz and Defense Secretary Caspar Weinberger insisted Bush attended one of the meetings where selling weapons to Iran was discussed. Bush said he was not at any such meeting. Who was telling the truth?

The United States Senate ordered an investigation. Texas Senator John Tower was placed in charge of the committee looking into the matter. After doing its research, the Tower Commission cleared Bush of any wrongdoing in the Iran-Contra scandal. Despite those findings, many Americans had doubts about Bush's innocence. Regardless, in the eyes of the law, he had a clean slate and could move on.

7

CAMPAIGN '88

B ush was looking forward to running for president in 1988. Overseas, there was good news. Soviet Union premier Mikhail Gorbachev was spearheading a reform movement, trying to make his gigantic nation more democratic.

What caused such drastic changes in the once dominant Soviet Union? Reagan's supporters said they were a result of the president's tough policies. Reagan opponents argued that the Soviets' corrupt and inefficient Communist dictatorship had weakened their country. Changes would have occurred regardless of who was president, they maintained. Still other observers conceded that it was a combination of both reasons.

In addition, the United States's economy was still strong, but with one major problem. The country was suffering a huge deficit. That was exactly what Bush had warned about in 1980 when he called Reagan's economic plan "voodoo economics."

There was another big question. Would voters not trust Bush because he may have had something to do with Iran-Contra? Early in 1988, surveys showed that a high number of Americans believed that Bush at least knew about Iran-Contra, even if he did not make any actual decisions involving the matter.[1]

It did not hurt him in the Republican primary elections. Bush coasted to the nomination. He chose Indiana Senator Dan Quayle as his running mate. George Bush and Dan Quayle faced the Democratic ticket of Massachusetts Governor Michael Dukakis and Texas Senator Lloyd

Bush chose Indiana Senator Dan Quayle as his running mate on the Republican ticket.

Bentsen, the same man who beat Bush in the Texas Senate race of 1970.

Bush made a vow to be the environmental president. The audience cheered Bush at the Republican National Convention in New Orleans when he promised that he would make America "a kinder, gentler, nation." That was in response to critics who said only the wealthy were enjoying prosperity under Reagan's economic policies.

Bush warned that a Dukakis presidency would lead to higher taxes and more expensive federal programs that would not work. He then made a bold promise by announcing firmly to the convention audience, "My opponent won't rule out raising taxes, but I will. And Congress will push me to raise taxes, and I'll say no, and they'll push, and I'll say no, and they'll push again. And I'll say to them: Read my lips. No new taxes!"[2]

The presidential campaign of 1988 is perceived by historians as one of the nastiest in modern history. By that summer, public opinion polls showed Dukakis with a lead of 18 percent over Bush.[3] At the Democratic National Convention in Atlanta, Senator Edward Kennedy from Massachusetts gave a speech linking Bush to Iran-Contra. He led the audiences in chants of "Where was George?" after he mentioned various wrongdoings related to the scandal. It was a powerful speech.[4]

What would Bush do to gain on Dukakis? He needed to rid himself of the "wimp" image. He was still viewed by many as a man who did not think for himself. Even George Will, a conservative Republican columnist, referred to Bush as Ronald Reagan's "lapdog."[5] Bush did not help himself by claiming, "I'm for Mr. Reagan blindly."[6] He defended himself by saying that loyalty was something to be proud of.

Bush's friend, General Brent Scowcroft conceded that the wimp name "hurt Bush's feelings a lot."[7] Scowcroft added, "It was based on an accusation that he didn't stand up for his thoughts. But he thought it was his job as vice president to support the president and not make his own policies."[8]

Bush's campaign emphasized his hard work in the Texas oil fields, certainly no place for wimps. His staff brought up his war record, and how he supported a strong defense. He even made references to his favorite snack, pork rinds, as a real man's food.

Then the Bush campaign went on the attack. Massachusetts had a weekend furlough program for convicted criminals. Prisoners were given a bit of freedom in the outside world as a means of rehabilitating them. The Bush campaign learned that an African-American prisoner, Willie Horton, escaped from his furlough and viciously attacked a family in another state. A group supporting Bush aired a television advertisement showing a photo of a vicious-looking Horton. The ad claimed that the furlough program proved that Dukakis was soft on crime.

What the ad did not say was that the furlough program had been started by the Republican governor who preceded Dukakis. Nor did it say that most states had similar programs. That included California when Ronald Reagan was its governor. The fact that Horton was African American made many believe that the Bush campaign was purposely exploiting racist fears some white people have. Even Bush's friend Brent Scowcroft admitted, "The Willie Horton ad played on people's fears. No question about that."[9] *Time* magazine insisted that Bush's staff was thrilled to link Dukakis to Horton.[10] In fact, a Bush campaign worker named Lee Atwater said one goal of the Bush campaign was to "make Willie Horton his (Dukakis's) running mate."[11]

The Bush campaign staff also learned that Dukakis refused to sign a bill which would have made it a criminal offense for a teacher not to lead his or her class in the Pledge of Allegiance each day. A group supporting Bush aired an advertisement implying that the Massachusetts governor was unpatriotic. Bush even visited a flag factory to emphasize his patriotism.

Dukakis said he refused to sign the bill because it was unconstitutional. He explained,

> I asked the Massachusetts Supreme Court for an advisory and they said it was unconstitutional to impose a criminal penalty on someone who refuses to salute the flag. It goes back to a case where Jehovah's Witnesses refused to salute the flag during World War II. They [Jehovah's Witnesses] cannot take an oath to anyone other than God. They [the Bush campaign staff] continually mischaracterized the bill.[12]

Was Bush's campaign dirty or clever? One who defended Bush's campaign was Ronald Reagan's press secretary Marlin Fitzwater. He said that Bush's visit to the flag factory was a justifiable response to Dukakis's rejection of the pledge of allegiance bill. He added that it was Dukakis's fellow Democrat, Senator Al Gore from Tennessee, who first raised the issue of the prison furlough program during the Democratic primary season.

Dukakis later noted that while Gore may have brought up the issue, the Bush campaign staff took advantage of it.

He stated that during the campaign, "The Republican state committee in Illinois put Willie Horton's picture on a brochure and distributed it all over the state. They were suggesting that your children will not be safe if Dukakis is elected."[13]

One other controversial anti-Dukakis advertisement became known as the "revolving door" ad. It ran on national television and showed criminals walking in circles through a revolving door. The ad seemed to be saying that unrehabilitated prisoners in Massachusetts were released into the public allowing them to commit more crimes. According to Dukakis, "It was all brown and black faces coming out of that revolving door."[14]

Surprisingly, Dukakis did not defend himself against these tactics until late in the campaign. He also refused to criticize Bush for any role he might have had in Iran-Contra.

Dukakis later confessed that was a mistake. He admitted, "I think I did a very poor job doing what you have to do, dealing with the attacks. I decided I'd just blow them off, but the lesson is that you can't do that. Ideally what you try to do is turn the other guy's attacks into a character issue on him, but it's easier said than done."[15]

Dukakis successfully used that strategy when he ran for governor of Massachusetts in 1982. So why did he not use it when running against Bush? He replied, "This was the presidency. I tried to keep it positive."[16]

Even with the negative campaigning, some observers say Americans were feeling too good in 1988 to make a change. Dukakis conceded that the election would have been very close, but he could have won. When the votes were counted on election day, November 8, 1988, George

When the votes were counted on election day, Bush was victorious. George Bush is shown here with his wife Barbara, and Ronald and Nancy Reagan.

Bush received 54 percent of the vote to 46 percent for Dukakis. He received 426 electoral votes to Dukakis's 112.[17] It was a commanding victory for Bush and Quayle.

Why did Bush win with such relative ease? According to Brent Scowcroft,

> I think it was a combination of his personality — a trusted personality, and that his opponent suffered by comparison in policy and personality. And Bush was by all odds probably the most prepared president we ever had with all his experience. And he was endorsed by a very popular president, Reagan.[18]

8

FAREWELL TO THE DICTATORS

Most of the nation was in high spirits when George Herbert Walker Bush was sworn into office on January 20, 1989. Republicans expected Bush's first term to almost be like a third term for Reagan. The enormous budget deficit still existed, but it seemed to be in the backs of most Americans' minds. A poll early in Bush's term showed him with an approval rating of 61 percent. By comparison, Ronald Reagan's approval rating at the beginning of his presidency was 55 percent.[1]

The first major issue President Bush tackled had nothing to do with usual issues, like the budget or foreign affairs. On June 21, 1989, the United States Supreme Court ruled that burning the American flag was a legal form of free speech. Bush could not have been more disappointed.[2] To Bush, flag burning went beyond making a statement. It was attacking a beloved symbol of the

United States. Bush called for an amendment to the United States Constitution making it illegal to desecrate the American flag.

Bush's critics said the president was "wrapping himself in the American flag," just to remain popular. Those who knew Bush emphasized his sincerity. Marlin Fitzwater, Bush's press secretary, said, "President Bush was strongly influenced his whole life by his service in World War II. His patriotism and respect for his country was very strong, as it was with most people of his generation. He saw the desecration of the American flag as a repulsive act."[3]

The first step to make an amendment become part of the Constitution is a vote in Congress. A total of two thirds

George Bush was sworn into office on January 20, 1989.

of the members of Congress must vote for it. Bush campaigned hard for the amendment.

At the same time, there was stirring news overseas. The Soviet reform movement was having a ripple effect. People of the eastern European nations under Communist control were taking to the streets to protest their governments. This was especially true in Czechoslovakia, Hungary, and Poland. Citizens and the police and troops representing the governments of these countries engaged in physical clashes.

Privately, Bush and his staff were thrilled with the fact that people were openly rebelling against Communism.[4] But in public, Bush did not show his real emotions. He did not want to embarrass the Soviet Union. If so, the Bush staff feared, the Soviets might take military action to stop the uprisings. In early fall, the Communist governments of Poland and Hungary were toppled.

In October, Bush received disappointing news. His anti-flag-burning amendment failed to pass the Senate by fifteen votes.[5] Both Republicans and Democrats voted against it. While many saw flag burning as a horrible act, they believed the government has no right to tell people they cannot do it.

Bush only had to look overseas to cheer up. By fall anti-Communist demonstrations had reached East Germany. The movement had even spread to what was perhaps Europe's strongest link to the Soviet Union, East Berlin.

Then, on November 9, 1989, the impossible happened. East Germany opened the Berlin Wall. The world's citizens had wondered if it would ever be opened in their lifetimes. Yet, to the anti-Communist demonstrators, it was not enough that the wall was open. With hammers and other tools, massive crowds of freedom-hungry Germans attacked the wall and literally tore it to pieces. They danced, sang, and cheered as the wall was destroyed.

Bush was at his desk when an adviser told him the news about the wall. The president immediately entered a nearby study, and, along with millions of people around the world, watched on television the happy throngs of people in Berlin. As excited as he was, Bush again kept cool in public.

He wrote,

> A wrong move could destroy the joy we were witnessing. Senator George Mitchell, Congressman Dick Gephardt, and other Democrats soon suggested that I go to Berlin to 'dance' on the Wall. This was pure foolishness. [West German leader Helmut] Kohl later told me how outrageously stupid such a move on my part would have been. It would have poured gasoline on the embers, an open provocation to the Soviet military to act.[6]

Other Communist governments began to crumble at a pace few could have imagined just a few months earlier. The day after the Berlin Wall fell, the Communist leader of Bulgaria resigned. On November 28, West German Chancellor Helmut Kohl announced a plan for reunifying Germany. On December 2 and 3, Bush and Gorbachev had a meeting on the island nation of Malta in the Mediterranean Sea. The leaders of the world's two largest powers were hoping to have a quiet get-together on the usually calm waters of the Mediterranean. Unfortunately, the worst storm in years struck the island, and the waters were anything but peaceful.

While the weather was rough, the spirit of the meeting was not. Gorbachev promised to avoid violent interference in countries rebelling against Communism, and Bush said the United States would keep its distance as well. Bush said, "We don't want to create big problems for you."[7] Then on December 5, another Communist government fell, as non-Communists took over the majority of the cabinet in Czechoslovakia.

While the situation in Europe was brightening, that was not the case in Bush's own hemisphere. The Central American country of Panama was ruled by dictator Manuel Noriega. Unlike the situation in eastern Europe, Communism was not the problem in Panama.

Noriega was highly suspected of trafficking in illegal

In 1989, crowds of Germans attacked the Berlin Wall, destroying it. Shown here is a piece of the wall.

drugs. In addition, he was ruling his country with an iron fist. Elections had been held in Panama. Noriega's opponents, Guillermo Endara and Guillermo "Billy" Ford, were elected president and vice president by the Panamanian people. But Noriega ruled that the elections did not count, and he remained in power. Ford was beaten senseless on the streets of Panama City by Noriega's armed soldiers. That image was broadcast around the world.

On December 16, an American marine in Panama who had gotten lost escaping a roadblock was shot by Noriega's soldiers. Shortly afterwards, another American marine and his wife were captured and tortured in Panama. With American lives at stake, Bush felt the time for action had come. Noriega had to be removed.

On December 17, Bush gathered his staff together to plan an American invasion of Panama. He wrote in his diary, "It's a major gamble," since he knew many governments in Central and South America, or Latin America, felt the United States should stay out of other Latin American countries' affairs.[8] But Bush was certain he was doing the right thing.

The attack was slated to take place at one o'clock in the morning on Wednesday, December 20. The action would be called "Operation Just Cause," because Bush believed it was a truly honorable effort.

On the evening of December 19, the Bushes held a Christmas reception. After the guests went home, the president told the first lady that Panama would be invaded the next day. She went to sleep, but the president stayed up until four o'clock A.M. Bush wrote in his diary, "So the tension mounts. They asked whether I would sleep; but there's no way I will be able to sleep;

SOURCE DOCUMENT

PRESIDENTIAL ANNOUNCEMENT

MY FELLOW CITIZENS: LAST NIGHT, I ORDERED U.S. MILITARY FORCES TO PANAMA. NO PRESIDENT TAKES SUCH ACTION LIGHTLY. THIS MORNING, I WANT TO TELL YOU WHAT I DID AND WHY I DID IT.

FOR NEARLY TWO YEARS THE UNITED STATES, THE NATIONS OF LATIN AMERICA AND THE CARIBBEAN, HAVE WORKED TOGETHER TO RESOLVE THE CRISIS IN PANAMA. THE GOALS OF THE U.S. HAVE BEEN TO SAFEGUARD THE LIVES OF AMERICANS, TO DEFEND DEMOCRACY IN PANAMA, TO COMBAT DRUG TRAFFICKING AND TO PROTECT THE INTEGRITY OF THE PANAMA CANAL TREATY.

2

MANY ATTEMPTS HAVE BEEN MADE TO RESOLVE THIS CRISIS THROUGH DIPLOMACY AND NEGOTIATIONS. ALL WERE REJECTED BY THE DICTATOR OF PANAMA, GENERAL MANUEL NORIEGA, AN INDICTED DRUG TRAFFICKER.

LAST FRIDAY, NORIEGA DECLARED HIS MILITARY DICTATORSHIP TO BE IN A STATE OF WAR WITH THE UNITED STATES AND PUBLICLY THREATENED THE LIVES OF AMERICANS IN PANAMA. THE VERY NEXT DAY, FORCES UNDER HIS COMMAND SHOT *and KILLED* AN UNARMED AMERICAN SERVICEMAN ~~TO DEATH~~, WOUNDED ANOTHER, ARRESTED AND BEAT A THIRD AMERICAN SERVICEMAN, *Brutally Interrogations* ~~AND THREATENED~~ HIS WIFE *and threatening her with sexual abuse. That was enough*

President Bush took these notes for his speech regarding the situation in Panama in December 1989.

during an operation of this nature where the lives of American kids are at risk. . . ."[9]

In the dark of night over Panama, a sky full of United States paratroopers descended on Panama City. After landing, they closed in on Noriega's headquarters building, the Comandancia, where they surrounded and captured Noriega's guards. Other American troops attacked the airport, including Noriega's Lear jet, so he could not leave his country.

At forty minutes after seven in the morning on December 20, Bush went on television to tell the American people why the military had just invaded Panama. Within twenty-four hours, most of the fighting had ended. A total of twenty-four Americans died in the fighting, but Endara and Ford were now Panama's president and vice president.[10] But where was Noriega?

For four days Noriega was nowhere to be found. Then, on Christmas Eve, he was spotted turning himself into the Vatican's embassy in Panama City. In the embassy he was protected from being arrested.

It was a truly busy time in world affairs, with history being made in all parts of the globe. Across the ocean, another Communist government fell. Perhaps the most oppressive of Communist leaders at the time, Nicolae Ceausescu, of Romania, was overthrown. On Christmas Day, Ceausescu and his wife were executed by rebellious Romanians. Just four days later, a playwright and champion of democracy named Vaclav Havel was elected president of the Czechoslovakian parliament.

Back in Panama, American troops did everything they could to get Noriega to surrender and face justice. They even played rock music outside the Vatican embassy, blasting songs with titles such as "Nowhere to Run," "I Fought the Law (And the Law Won)," and "You're No Good." On January 3, 1990, embassy officials convinced Noriega to give up. He did so, and Panamanians danced in the streets with joy. The next morning, Noriega was flown to Miami, Florida, where he was placed under arrest on charges of drug-trafficking. A poll taken by CBS television news showed that nine out of ten Panamanians supported Operation Just Cause.[11]

That was not the case with other countries. The United Nations, with its large Third World membership, officially condemned the United States action. So did the Organization of American States (OAS), a similar group of nations located in the Western Hemisphere. However, there was very little damage to the United States by these condemnations. Bush's National Security Advisor Brent Scowcroft said that "was due to Noriega being a very unsavory character. And President Bush had spoken to all the Latin American heads of state before the military action."[12]

Scowcroft also speculated that the actions of the UN and OAS were formalities. They publicly condemned the United States actions just to let the world know they generally do not approve of intervention in Latin America countries. Scowcroft added that many of these nations which had condemned the United States were privately happy to see Noriega out of office.[13] At home, Bush received praise from Democrats and Republicans alike.

Why was the invasion so successful? Marlin Fitzwater replied, "We didn't rush into it right away. It was a build-up over time. It allowed Latin American countries time so they could see Noreiga was a real outlaw. They saw pictures of [his soldiers] beating up Billy Ford."[14]

Brent Scowcroft added, "Noriega was not particularly liked by the Panamanian people. He clearly stole the election by stopping the vote counting. And we had a duly elected administration to put in place after we kicked out Noriega."[15]

As a new decade got underway, the beginnings of what was being called a New World Order were firmly in place. And President Bush seemed to be on top of the world.

9

PROMISES, PROMISES

A t first glance, Barbara Bush seemed one of the least likely first ladies to be the subject of a controversy. She contrasted greatly with the previous first lady. Nancy Reagan, a former actress, was slender and glamorous. She was also widely attacked for being more interested in acquiring fancy possessions and dressing well than helping others.

No one could say that of Barbara Bush. No longer the slender brown-haired girl of her youth, her hair had grown white. She had a portly build and appeared matronly. Since the president was still boyish-looking with a full head of brown hair, comedians joked about her looking more like President Bush's mother than his wife. She took it all in stride. Once she even wisecracked to a reporter saying that she refused to turn down a piece of cake since losing weight would hurt her image.

As first lady, Barbara Bush worked hard to fight illiteracy in America. She often visited schools where she read to children, and she helped raise funds for groups combating illiteracy.

In spring of 1990, Barbara Bush was invited to speak at the June 1 graduation ceremony at all-female Wellesley College in Massachusetts. Since Mikhail Gorbachev and his wife Raisa were to be in Washington for a meeting at the same time, Barbara invited Raisa to make a speech with her. Hearing the wives of two world leaders would seem to be a special opportunity for the Wellesley graduates.

But not all Wellesley seniors felt that way. About one hundred fifty of the six hundred graduates signed a petition urging Wellesley to hire another speaker. They said Barbara Bush did not accomplish anything on her own, but was well-known only because she was married to a famous man. The petition read in part that Wellesley "teaches us that we will be rewarded on the basis of our own merit, not on that of a spouse."[1]

In response, the first lady received a huge amount of support from people who felt her crusade against illiteracy was something she did achieve on her own. Barbara Bush and Raisa Gorbachev both spoke as scheduled. Near the end of her talk, Barbara said, "And who knows? Somewhere out in this audience may even be someone who will one day follow in my footsteps, and preside over the White House as the President's spouse. I wish him well!"[2]

As she finished that line of her speech, the women graduates let out a roar of approval and burst into a huge round of applause.

The president had his own favorite cause, the Points of Light Foundation. The idea for the foundation stemmed from basic conservative beliefs that volunteerism works better than government programs. The group consisted of people who contributed to their communities for no monetary or other reward. On one occasion, Bush told a group of United States Marines who volunteered with school children, "On every single day of the year except Sunday, I name as a Point of Light a person or group serving their community somewhere in America, volunteers helping other people. I call them our Points of Light because their caring deeds shine like beacons of hope."[3]

The president still had his share of critics. They said he failed to live up to his promise of creating a kinder, gentler nation when on June 29, 1990, he vetoed the Family and Medical Leave Act of 1990. A veto is the right of a president to refuse to sign a bill passed by Congress.

This act would have made it a requirement for businesses to allow their workers to take time off from their jobs to care for a new baby or a sick relative. Companies would not have to pay workers during that time. This policy is in place in much of Europe.

The Republican party had claimed to be the party of family values. Bush's opponents asked what kind of family values Bush had by vetoing this act. Bush responded, "I want to emphasize my belief that time off for a child's birth or adoption or for family illness is an important benefit for employers to offer employees. I strongly object, however, to the Federal Government mandating leave policies for America's employers and work force."[4]

The same day Bush held a press conference where he appeared to break another campaign promise. As many expected, the federal deficit had grown so deep that Bush announced he would have to raise taxes or start new ones.

Without hesitating, reporters challenged him on not keeping his word. When one journalist asked the president if this would cause people not to believe him, Bush answered, "Look, I knew I'd catch some flak on this decision. But I've got to do what I think is right, and then I'll ask the people for support."[5]

Most Americans did not think it was right. Many believed Bush made a promise he knew he could not keep to get elected. Even *The New York Post*, a newspaper with a conservative Republican editorial policy, blasted across the front page, "READ MY LIPS — I LIED."[6] Bush's press secretary Marlin Fitzwater later said, "It was definitely a mistake. People held it against him for breaking his promise."[7] A joke among Democrats went, "They told me if I voted for Dukakis my taxes would go up. They were right. I voted for Dukakis and my taxes went up."

Dukakis himself said that Bush had no intention of keeping his promise. He said that he and Bush met shortly after the 1988 election in a friendly get-together. The purpose was to discuss ways of reducing the deficit. According to Dukakis, "He [Bush] said to me, 'If I raise taxes in my first year they'll kill me.' I almost fell off my chair. I said to myself this guy will not keep his commitment. And when did he raise taxes?"[8]

However, Bush's National Security Advisor Brent Scowcroft said that Bush did have every intention of keeping the promise not to raise taxes. He said Bush's only mistake was making the promise in such definite terms.[9]

To Republicans, much of the blame for the economy

went to the Democrat-controlled Congress. Marlin Fitzwater stated that the Senate majority leader, Democratic Senator George Mitchell of Maine, did not cooperate with Senate Republicans. According to Fitzwater, "It [raising taxes] was probably also a mistake economically. We didn't get the spending reductions along with it. In hindsight, Bush should have said, 'The Democrats and George Mitchell won't give us anything and we're trying.'"[10]

The media greatly attacked Bush for going back on his promise. To conservatives, Bush's real mistake was not breaking a campaign promise but raising taxes. A basic conservative rule of thought is that higher taxes rarely solve economic problems.

Things went a bit smoother for Bush over the rest of the year. In July, Bush nominated a little known New Hampshire judge named David Souter to fill a vacancy on the United States Supreme Court. Souter was overwhelmingly confirmed by Congress.

Then, on July 26, Bush signed the landmark Americans with Disabilities Act of 1990. It banned discrimination against people with mental or physical impairments. It added that people whose conditions were due to illegal drug use were not covered. Bush announced, "With today's signing of the landmark Americans for [sic] Disabilities Act, every man, woman, and child with a disability can now pass through once-closed doors into a bright new era of quality, independence, and freedom."[11] To Marlin Fitzwater, the act was "the most defining moment, domestically, of Bush's administration. It was the last great civil rights bill, a far-sighted piece of legislation."[12]

In August, Iraq invaded Kuwait, and the events in the Persian Gulf region occupied Americans' minds. But at home, Bush had a campaign promise he wanted to fulfill—to be the environmental president. On November 15, he signed a bill amending the Clean Air Act of 1970. The amendment put limits on the amounts of pollutants such as ozone, carbon monoxide, lead, and sulphur dioxide that factories could release into the air. Its goal was to reduce air pollution each year by 56 billion pounds, which equaled 224 pounds for each American citizen within fifteen years.[13]

As he signed the bill, Bush discussed a trip he recently had taken to Camp David, a presidential retreat in the mountains of Maryland. He said, "Saturday and Sunday really were fantastic—clear and crisp and beautiful, bright sunshine and those magnificent fall colors. And it was great to get out in the woods. But no American should have to drive out of town to breathe clean air. Every city in America should have clean air. And with this legislation, I firmly believe we will."[14]

The next day he signed two similar laws. One helped protect the environment of Antarctica. The purpose of the other was to control water pollution in the Great Lakes.

After the Persian Gulf War ended, a poll showed Bush with an unheard of approval rating of 89 percent.[15] Those who fought in the war were honored with a parade in New York City. There was other thrilling news from the Middle East. All the remaining hostages in Lebanon, who were at the root of the Iran-Contra scandal, were gradually released until all were safe at home.

But the happenings in the Middle East quickly faded into Americans' memories as they became more and more concerned about the economy. Some workers lost jobs. Others saw their incomes either drop or not keep up with the cost of living. They increasingly blamed Bush's leadership.

As if these headaches were not enough, in early May Bush was diagnosed with Graves' disease. It is a condition caused by the body producing too much thyroid hormone. The first lady had suffered from the same illness in 1989, but Bush's case affected the rhythm of his heart. In just months, Bush went from being on top of the world to a man with a bundle of problems.

Bush and Gorbachev met one more time. On July 31, the two leaders signed a treaty to reduce each nation's nuclear weapons. It was called the Strategic Arms Reduction Treaty or START. It decreed that each country would reduce its stockpile of nuclear weapons roughly 30 percent over the course of seven years.[16]

Just weeks later, on August 17, Bush was vacationing in Kennebunkport, Maine, when he received some frightening news. As rain from a hurricane pounded the roof of his home, he received a phone call from Brent Scowcroft. Scowcroft announced that there had a been a coup, or military takeover, in the former Soviet Union. Reports said that Gorbachev was out and a Communist leader named Gennadi Yanayev had taken over the government.

The hurricane passed after doing only minor damage. The same could be said of the takeover. The Communist rebels were ill-prepared. At one point the president of the Republic of Russia and a former Communist, Boris Yeltsin, climbed atop a tank rallying Moscow's residents behind him. By this action, Yeltsin showed the rebels that he was strong and in control.

Marlin Fitzwater remembered, "It has been said that when they [the rebels] were inside the Kremlin [the Soviet seat of government] they were watching [the cable television news network] CNN and saw Bush saying that not all coups succeed. That made them start to consider that the coup could unravel."[17]

In three days, the coup was over. Yayanev was arrested shortly afterwards. Although Gorbachev had survived, he was severely weakened. Several of the Soviet republics seized the moment to declare independence from the Soviet Union. Gorbachev stepped down as head of the Communist party, although he continued as his country's president. On August 29, the Soviet parliament banned all Communist party activities. After seventy-four years as a world power, the Soviet Union was on its last legs.

While Bush kept an eye on the situation overseas, an unusual occurrence was taking place at home. Thurgood Marshall, the only African American on the United States Supreme Court and a liberal, resigned. In Kennebunkport, Bush named the man he had chosen to replace Marshall. He was a conservative African-American judge named Clarence Thomas. Unlike David Souter, Thomas would not be easily confirmed.

A woman named Anita Hill who had worked under Thomas accused the judge of sexually harassing her many times. Just fifteen years earlier, sexual harassment did not exist as a legal issue. The problem was brought into the public eye by the National Organization for Women (NOW) and other feminist groups. If Thomas was guilty, he would not be suited for a position as Supreme Court justice. Thomas flatly denied the charges and hearings were held to see who was telling the truth. It basically came down to Thomas's word against Hill's. Feminists and liberals supported Anita Hill while conservatives sided with Thomas.

Bush stood by his appointee 100 percent. In a letter to a friend in Texas, he wrote, "What is happening to Clarence Thomas is just plain horrible. . . . They are trying to destroy this decent man."[18] In the end, Thomas was confirmed as Supreme Court justice, but by a slim margin of four votes.

Meanwhile, the Soviet Union continued unraveling. As when the Iron Curtain countries of eastern Europe rallied against Communism, Bush refused to gloat. On Christmas

In 1991, Boris Yeltsin (left), shown here with President Bush and his wife Barbara, became the new leader of the former Soviet Union.

Day, 1991, Gorbachev resigned as president of the Soviet Union. The Soviet Union, once feared by much of the world, ceased to exist. Boris Yeltsin was the new leader of a non-Communist union which replaced the Soviet Union. He called it the Commonwealth of Independent States.

10

"NOT THE POSITION I WOULD HAVE PREFERRED"

Although Americans were thrilled with the news from the former Soviet Union, that did not translate into support for Bush. In fact, in early January 1992, Bush made headlines for an embarrassing accident. While at a formal dinner in Japan, Bush became sick and vomited all over the Japanese prime minister, Kiichi Miyazawa.

Television coverage showed the ill American president being held by Miyazawa. *Time* magazine reported that the image was a symbol of the American economy: "flat on its back, seeking succor [or relief] from a resurgent Japan."[1] A number of Japanese companies had been buying American businesses and many in the United States felt threatened by that trend.

The president spent much of 1992 campaigning for a second term as president. The only other major

SOURCE DOCUMENT

IMPORTANT ANNOUNCEMENT

February 6, 1992

THIS IS AN ALL POINTS BULLETIN FROM THE PRESIDENT *GB/*

SUBJECT: MY DOG "RANGER"

Recently Ranger was put on a weight reduction program. Either that program succeeds or we enter Ranger in the Houston Fat Stock Show as a Prime Hereford.

All offices Should take a formal 'pledge' that reads as follows:

"WE AGREE NOT TO FEED RANGER.WE WILL NOT GIVE HIM BISCUITS.WE WILL NOT GIVE HIM FOOD OF ANY KIND"

In addition Ranger's "access" is hereby restricted. He has been told not to wander the corridors without an escort. This applies to the East and West Wings, to the Residence from the 3rd floor to the very, very bottom basement.

Although Ranger will still be permitted to roam at Camp David, the Camp David staff including Marines, Naval Personnel, All Civilians and Kids are specifically instructed to 'rat' on anyone seen feeding Ranger.

Ranger has been asked to wear a "Do not feed me" badge in addition to his ID.

I will, of course, report on Ranger's fight against obesity. Right now he looks like a blimp, a nice friendly appealing blimp, but a blimp.

We need Your Help- All hands, please, help.

FROM THE PRESIDENT

Although Bush was being criticized in the press, he still managed to keep his sense of humor. Here is a memo he sent out to his office staff.

Republican candidate to challenge him for the party's nomination was ultraconservative columnist Pat Buchanan. Although Bush won the New Hampshire primary, Buchanan made a strong showing. He won 37 percent of the vote, just sixteen points less than Bush.[2] Bush won enough primaries and caucuses to win his party's nomination, but Buchanan had to be taken very seriously.

That June, Bush headed to Rio de Janeiro, Brazil, for a unique meeting. It was officially titled the United Nations Conference on Environment and Development (UNCED), but most people called it the Earth Summit. A total of 170 nations, nearly all in the world, were represented.[3] In attendance were over one hundred heads of state.[4] The purpose was a difficult one: for the nations of the world to work together to better protect the earth.

The United States signed one treaty at the conference. Its intent was to reduce carbon dioxide emissions to fight global warming. However, the United States refused to sign a second treaty which was to help keep a diverse array of species alive. Bush said one reason he did not sign it was that it did not protect American drug companies which get genetic information from some tropical species. Another reason was the expense. In support of her husband, the first lady said it would have cost the United States billions of dollars.[5]

Bush took hard hits from environmentalists. They believed the costs were not that high. To them, Bush was not the environmental president he claimed to be.

The president told reporters at the conference,

> Let me be clear on one fundamental point. The United States fully intends to be the world's preeminent leader

> in protecting the global environment. . . . And the fact
> that we don't go along with every single covenant, I
> don't think that means a relinquishment of leadership. I
> think we are, and I think the record shows we are, the
> leading environmental nation in the world.[6]

The National Republican Convention took place two months later in August in New Orleans. Because Pat Buchanan did so well during the primary season, he was permitted to give a speech. Many Republicans were uneasy about giving Buchanan an open platform. They had good reason. In a speech some branded hateful, Buchanan openly criticized immigrants and homosexuals. Most moderate Republicans did not share Buchanan's points of view. To them it was disturbing that their party should become so extreme.

By this time, there were signs that the economy was improving. There was a 5 percent growth in the last two quarters of 1992.[7] But was it a case of too little, too late?

In his campaign, Bush went on the attack, as he did against Dukakis in 1988. At one point he even resorted to calling Democratic presidential nominee Bill Clinton and his running mate Al Gore "bozos."[8]

When the candidates debated in person, Clinton looked lively and ready to take on any challenge. Bush appeared to be tired and worn out. During one debate, Bush was seen on television checking the time on his watch. It seemed as if he was weary and could not wait for the campaign to end. He also attacked Clinton's sense of patriotism. Clinton was one of thousands of young men who publicly demonstrated against the Vietnam War and did not serve in it. Some say he purposely evaded the draft.

In the first debate in St. Louis, Bush referred to Clinton when he said, "I was 19 or 20 flying off an aircraft carrier and that shaped me to be Commander-in-Chief of the armed forces and I'm sorry, but demonstrating — it's not a question of patriotism. It's a question of character and judgment."[9]

Unlike Dukakis, Clinton was ready with a response. He made it personal as he told Bush,

> When Joe McCarthy went around this country attacking people's patriotism he was wrong. He was wrong. And a senator from Connecticut stood up to him named Prescott Bush. Your father was right to stand up to Joe McCarthy, you were wrong to attack my patriotism. I was opposed to the war but I loved my country and we need a president who will bring this country together, not divide it.[10]

Michael Dukakis recalled, "He stopped Bush dead in his tracks. It was like he hit Bush between the eyes with a two by four."[11]

Breaking his campaign promise about not raising taxes was a serious issue. Bush was routinely mocked for it. For example, those attending a pro-Clinton "Read My Lips" rally in Keene, New Hampshire, were handed big, fake, red lips to wear.

That year, there was also a third-party candidate for president. Billionaire businessman H. Ross Perot ran as an independent. Perot seemed to be drawing more Republicans than Democrats, which hurt Bush in the polls. But as the campaign wound down towards the last week-end, Bush was closing the gap with Clinton. Some polls had the race as dead even between Clinton and Bush, with Perot trailing behind.

Then, just before the election, a bombshell was dropped. Little had been mentioned during the campaign of any possible role Bush may have had in the Iran-Contra Affair. On Friday, October 30, Iran-Contra special prosecutor Lawrence E. Walsh issued a one-count indictment [a charge of a criminal wrongdoing] against Reagan's former defense secretary Caspar Weinberger. It raised questions once more about Bush's meetings with Weinberger and how much Bush knew about the whole affair.

On Tuesday, November 3, the American people voted and Bill Clinton was elected forty-second president of the United States. He received 357 electoral votes to Bush's 168. Clinton picked up 43 percent of the votes to Bush's 38. Perot won no electoral votes, but did earn 19 percent of the total.[12]

Bush blamed the Iran-Contra indictment on killing his momentum.[13] Marlin Fitzwater reacted even more strongly by saying, "I think the indictment was outrageous and perhaps a federal crime. The independent counsel was trying to interfere with the election."[14]

After the election, some members of the media said Bush did not have his heart in the campaign. But Fitzwater stated, "He's the most competitive person I've ever seen in my life. Doctors said the medication he was taking for Graves' Disease may have had some effect on his stamina. It may have affected his energy level. I don't think there was any lapse in heart and mind, but there was one in body."[15]

Michael Dukakis said Bush lost for two reasons. He noted, "For reasons I don't understand, Bush never seemed to be able to communicate his concern to people. People saw him tootling around Kennebunkport in that

On March 25, 1997, Bush recreated his World War II heroics by parachuting from an airplane.

motorboat while people said, 'We're hurting.' And he had no coherent plan to get the economy moving, like public works or cutting interest rates."[16]

Brent Scowcroft had his own theories about Bush's failure to be reelected. He noted, "A lot of Republicans thought we didn't have to fight hard to win the election after the victory in the Gulf War. And Clinton is an awesome campaigner. I don't know if anyone could have beaten him."[17]

On November 7, Bush addressed the American people in a radio address. He stated, "Way back in 1945, [British prime minister] Winston Churchill was defeated at the polls. He said, 'I have been given the Order of the Boot.' That is the exact same position in which I find myself today.

"I admit, this is not the position I would have preferred, but it is a judgment I honor. Having known the sweet taste of popular favor, I can more readily accept the sour taste of defeat, because it is seasoned for me by my deep devotion to the political system under which this Nation has thrived for two centuries."[18]

Bush was president for two more months. In late November, the United Nations requested help from the United States regarding a situation in the African country of Somalia. People there were starving as a result of civil war. Bush agreed something had to be done. On December 8, 1992, he sent American troops to Somalia in what was called Operation Restore Hope.

He also continued to hold meetings with world leaders. Bush, Canadian Prime Minister Brian Mulroney, and Mexican President Carlos Salinas de Gortari met on December 17 to sign the North American Free Trade Agreement (NAFTA). It would remove taxes called tariffs on imported items, allowing each country's citizens cheaper access to other countries' products. Congress would still need to vote to accept NAFTA before it became law.

Then, on January 3, 1993, Bush and Boris Yeltsin signed another arms reduction treaty, known as START II. One part of the treaty called for the elimination of all Intercontinental Ballistic Missiles (ICBMs). The first lady was proud to praise her husband's part in the treaty, and referred to ICBMs as "the dreadful rockets that had scared the wits out of generations of kids all over the world."[19]

In a controversial move days before he left office,

Bush pardoned Caspar Weinberger and several other Iran-Contra figures. That meant they could not be punished for any crimes they had committed during any events relating to Iran-Contra. On January 20, he passed the torch of leadership to Bill Clinton.

Bush spends his time in retirement in his homes in Houston and Kennebunkport. In 1997, he celebrated two singular events. On March 25, he recreated his World War II heroics by jumping from an airplane and parachuting to earth. On November 6, the George Bush Presidential Library and Museum was dedicated on the campus of Texas A&M University in College Station, Texas. About

On November 6, 1997, the George Bush Presidential Library and Museum was dedicated on the campus of Texas A&M University.

twenty thousand people were in attendance to honor the forty-first president.[20]

Bush paraphrased baseball legend Lou Gehrig as he spoke to the audience. With his voice cracking, he said, "Today, I feel like the luckiest person in the world."[21] Bush added, "Now that my political days are over, I can honestly say that the three most rewarding titles bestowed upon me are the three that I've got left — a husband, a father and a granddad."[22]

In attendance were former presidents Jimmy Carter and Gerald Ford, sitting president Bill Clinton, their wives and former first ladies Nancy Reagan and Lady Bird Johnson. Clinton, the man who defeated Bush, said, "You know, we have an interesting country with a lot of religious, racial and political divisions. Once in a while, we all get together. This morning, I think it's fair to say that all Americans are united in tribute to President George Bush for his lifetime of service to America."[23]

11

LEGACY

T o many Americans, George Bush's legacy is his family name. In 1994, his son George W. Bush was elected governor of Texas. In 1998, his son Jeb Bush was elected governor of Florida. Then in a very close election, George W. Bush was elected president of the United States in 2000. Three generations in high public office have made the Bushes of New England and Texas a true political dynasty.

But what about George Herbert Walker Bush's individual legacy as president? It takes years for a president's impact on history to be firmly established. For example, when Harry S. Truman and Dwight D. Eisenhower left office, they were ranked by historians as poor presidents. Today historians rank them among the best.

A poll taken of over seven hundred historians, politicians, and news commentators in 1997 ranked Bush in the middle of the average category. Out of forty-one presidents, he ranked twenty-second.[1] The poll was discussed at length in a book called *Rating the Presidents* by William J. Ridings and Stuart B. McIver. Ridings and McIver wrote, "In rating Bush twenty-second, poll participants play it safe, placing him in the middle third of American presidents, possibly an admission that they think it is too early to evaluate the performance of recent chief executives."[2]

A similar but smaller poll was taken in 1999 by the public affairs cable network, C-SPAN. In that poll, fifty-eight "historians and academics" were asked to rank the presidents in order of greatness.[3] In that poll Bush finished a bit better, ranking twentieth.[4]

While most Americans remember the Bush administration best for the victory in the Gulf War, not all experts believe that in itself was its most important event. In fact, some believe the war was a failure in that Iraqi dictator Saddam Hussein remained in power. The war's tenth anniversary was commemorated in the winter of 2001. At that time, a military history professor named Roger J. Spiller wrote, "Hussein survived and revived, and two presidents later, he still rules in Baghdad. If he did not win control over the oil he wanted, neither did he lose control over his country."[5]

Was the war not a total victory because the United States and the other United Nations forces did not remove Saddam Hussein from power? Many military experts agree with General Brent Scowcroft, Bush's national security advisor. Scowcroft said,

> Would I do anything differently? No. We did what the U.N. mandate asked us to do. We would have set an

unfortunate pattern in our behavior if we occupied Baghdad. We would be seen as not operating in the true nature of the United Nations, and acting in our own narrow interests. Were we to go into Baghdad, we would have been [viewed as] hated occupiers of a complex country. In addition, it's also important to note that if we continued into Baghdad, the coalition [of Arab nations] would have broken up.[6]

Scowcroft admitted that the conclusion of the Gulf War was the Bush administration's shining moment. However, he concedes that the most defining moment was "the day the hammer and sickle came down from the Kremlin [the capital of the former Soviet Union]."[7]

However, Scowcroft acknowledged that Bush is just one of a long line of presidents who deserve credit for

This exhibit on the Gulf War is on display at the George Bush Presidential Library and Museum.

bringing down the Communist empire. He said, "the credit basically goes to a series of American presidents, starting with Truman, who kept pressure on the Soviet Union and held this aggressive nation at bay. More than anything, the credit goes to Gorbachev. If it had been another Stalinist-like figure, like [Leonid] Brezhnev, we might still be in a cold war today."[8] Josef Stalin was a Communist dictator of the Soviet Union during World War II, and Leonid Brezhnev was a strong Communist Soviet leader from 1964 to 1982.

On the other hand, Bush's former press secretary Marlin Fitzwater gave most credit for the fall of European Communism to Ronald Reagan. Fitzwater said Bush's most shining moment was not the Gulf War itself, but what happened as a result of the desert conflict. Fitzwater noted, "For the first time, Americans sensed a pride in the military they hadn't experienced since Vietnam. The country felt better than it had in thirty-five or forty years, with the way the men and women coming home from the Gulf at the end of the war were received. There were parades and celebrations"[9]

Fitzwater also believes the Gulf War victory was a major step towards treaties Arab leaders signed with Israel during Bill Clinton's administration. He stated, "One outgrowth of the Persian Gulf War was that Arab countries agreed to recognize the independence of Israel and to denounce state-sponsored terrorism. There was a new relationship between the Arab world and the United States. The United States was now seen as a trusted ally."[10]

Fitzwater believes, too, that the Clean Air Act and the Americans with Disabilities Act were among the great accomplishments of the Bush presidency. Even Bush's opponent and critic, former Democratic presidential nominee Michael Dukakis, gave Bush high marks for those domestic policies.[11]

The Americans with Disabilities Act made headlines in 2001 for a highly publicized case decided by the United States Supreme Court. A talented golfer named Casey Martin wanted to play on the Professional Golf Association (PGA) tour. While his golfing skills qualified him for the tour, Martin suffered from a circulatory disorder in his legs that made it difficult to walk. The only way he could make it through an eighteen-hole golf course was by riding in a golf cart, which was forbidden by PGA rules.

Visitors to the exhibit on Bush's White House years at the Presidential Library and Museum can explore the many events that occurred while Bush was in office.

The Supreme Court ruled in Martin's favor. Martin announced, "Without the ADA, I never would have been able to pursue my dream of playing golf professionally."[12]

Unlike Scowcroft and Fitzwater, Dukakis gave Bush a mixed review concerning his legacy. Dukakis said, "The negative was his inability to come to grips with the economic decline. On the plus side, there is no question he was much better at foreign policy than domestic policy. You have to give him credit for his handling of the Gulf War and his strong performance handling the end of the Cold War."[13]

Some Bush supporters, like Brent Scowcroft, credit him for setting the stage for an economic boom which took place during the Clinton administration. For example, the NAFTA agreement, which Bush signed shortly before he left office, was passed by Congress during Clinton's first term.

So what is the legacy of George Herbert Walker Bush's presidency? Republicans give him high marks. Democrats give him mixed or low marks. As far as a consensus, time will tell.

Chronology

1924—Born in Milton, Massachusetts, on June 12 to Prescott Sheldon Bush and Dorothy Walker Bush; moves with family to Greenwich, Connecticut, at six months old.

1937—Attends Phillips Andover Academy in Andover, Massachusetts.

1942—Graduates Phillips Andover Academy; enlists in United States Navy to fight in World War II.

1944—Flies first mission on May 23; shot down over Chichi Jima by Japanese on September 2, then rescued.

1945—Marries Barbara Pierce on January 6; enrolls at Yale University in September.

1946—Son George Walker Bush born.

1948—Plays baseball in College World Series; graduates Yale; moves to Odessa, Texas, to work for Dresser Industries, a large oil supply company.

1949—Moves to southern California as part of job; daughter Pauline Robinson (Robin) Bush born.

1950—Moves to Midland, Texas, as part of promotion with Dresser Industries.

1951—Forms with a partner Bush-Overbey Oil Development Company, Inc.

1952—Father Prescott Bush elected to United States Senate from Connecticut.

1953—Son John Ellis (Jeb) Bush born; daughter Robin dies from leukemia; forms separate business, Zapata Petroleum.

1955—Son Neil Mallon Bush born.

1956—Son Marvin Pierce Bush born; new business division, Zapata Off-Shore, begins.

1959—Moves with family to Houston, Texas; daughter Dorothy Walker Bush born.

1962—Takes first political job with Republican Candidates Selection Committee in Harris County, Texas.

1964—Loses race for United States Senate.

1966—Sells Zapata Off-Shore; elected to United States House of Representatives.

1968—Reelected to United States House of Representatives.

1970—Loses second race for United States Senate.

1971—Appointed United States ambassador to United Nations.

1973—Appointed chairman of Republican National Committee.

1974—Appointed liaison officer to People's Republic of China.

1976—Appointed director of Central Intelligence Agency.

1977—Enters banking business after Democrat Jimmy Carter wins White House.

1979—Announces candidacy for president of the United States on May 1.

1980—Wins election as vice president under Ronald Reagan.

1984—Reelected vice president under Ronald Reagan.

1986—Iran-Contra scandal becomes public.

1988—Elected president of the United States.

1989—Flag desecration amendment rejected; Berlin Wall falls; sends troops to Panama.

1990—Vetoes Family and Medical Leave Act; raises taxes; signs Americans with Disabilities Act; Iraq invades Kuwait; signs amendment to Clean Air Act of 1970.

1991—Persian Gulf War; START treaty signed; Clarence Thomas controversy; Soviet Union dissolves.

1992—Loses bid for reelection to Bill Clinton; sends troops to Somalia; NAFTA agreement signed with Canada and Mexico.

1993—START II treaty signed; pardons Caspar Weinberger and other Iran-Contra figures.

1997—Parachutes from airplane to recreate World War II act; presidential library opens.

Chapter Notes

Chapter 1. Storm in the Desert
1. Herbert S. Parmet, *George Bush: The Life of a Lone Star Yankee* (New Brunswick, N.J.: Transaction Publishers, 2001), p. 481.

2. Colin Powell with Joseph E. Persico, *My American Journey* (New York: Random House, 1995), p. 508.

3. George Bush, *All The Best: My Life in Letters and Other Writings* (New York: A Lisa Drew Book, Charles Scribner's Sons, 1999), p. 513.

4. Powell, p. 518.

5. Ibid., p. 521.

6. "Address to the Nation on the Suspension of Allied Offensive Combat Operations in the Persian Gulf," Bush Library presidential papers, February 27, 1991, <http://bushlibrary.tamu.edu/papers/1991/91022702.htm> (June 22, 2001).

Chapter 2. "Have Half"
1. Fitzhugh Green, *Booknotes*, January 21, 1990 transcript <http://www.booknotes.org/Transcript/?ProgramID=1454&QueryText=fitzhugh+green> (March 14, 2001).

2. Herbert S. Parmet, *George Bush: The Life of a Lone Star Yankee* (New Brunswick, N.J.: Transaction Publishers, 2001), p. 34.

3. Ibid., p. 37.

4. Ibid., p. 39.

5. Fitzhugh Green, *George Bush: An Intimate Portrait* (New York: Hippocrene Books, 1989), p. 24.

6. Randall Rothenberg, "In Search of George Bush," *The New York Times Magazine*, March 6, 1988, p. 30.

Chapter 3. Off the Waters of Chichi Jima

1. Craig Haffner, executive producer, *Biography*, "George Bush: His World War II Years," Greystone Communications, Inc. and the Arts & Entertainment Network, 1992.

2. Joe Hyams, *Flight of the Avenger* (New York: Harcourt Brace Jovanovich Publications, 1991), p. 33.

3. Haffner.

4. George Bush, *All The Best: My Life in Letters and Other Writings* (New York: A Lisa Drew Book, Charles Scribner's Sons, 1999), p. 33.

5. Hyams, p. 54.

6. Ibid., p. 61.

7. Haffner.

8. Ibid.

9. Ibid.

10. Ibid.

11. Hyams, p. 84.

12. Ibid.

13. Patricia Burchfield and Jason Hancock, *George Bush: Presidential Library and Museum* (Lawrenceburg, Ind.: The Creative Company, 1999), p. 4.

14. Hyams, p. 156.

Chapter 4. Black Gold

1. Fitzhugh Green, *George Bush: An Intimate Portrait* (New York: Hippocrene Books, 1989), p. 44.

2. Patricia Burchfield and Jason Hancock, *George Bush: Presidential Library and Museum* (Lawrenceburg, Ind.: The Creative Company, 1999), p. 7.

3. George Bush, *All The Best: My Life in Letters and Other Writings* (New York: A Lisa Drew Book, Charles Scribner's Sons, 1999), p. 67.

4. George Bush with Victor Gold, *Looking Forward* (New York: Doubleday, 1987), p. 23.

5. Green, p. 58.

6. Burchfield and Hancock, p. 8.

7. Green, p. 65.

8. Barbara Bush, *Barbara Bush: A Memoir* (New York: A Lisa Drew Book, Charles Scribner's Sons, 1994), p. 46.

9. Ibid., p. 52.

Chapter 5. Goodbye Zapata, Hello Washington

1. Fitzhugh Green, *George Bush: An Intimate Portrait* (New York: Hippocrene Books, 1989), p. 87.

2. Public Broadcasting Co., "Campaign: The Choice," November 24, 1988.

3. Patricia Burchfield and Jason Hancock, *George Bush: Presidential Library and Museum* (Lawrenceburg, Ind.: The Creative Company, 1999), p. 10.

4. Randall Rothenberg, "In Search of George Bush," *The New York Times Magazine*, March 6, 1988, p. 46.

5. Ibid.

6. Garry Wills, "The Ultimate Loyalist," *Time*, August 22, 1988, p. 26.

7. Green, p. 114, and Herbert Parmet, *George Bush: The Life of a Lone Star Yankee* (New York: A Lisa Drew Book, Charles Scribner's Sons, 1997), p. 145.

8. George Bush, *All The Best: My Life in Letters and Other Writings* (New York: A Lisa Drew Book, Charles Scribner's Sons, 1999), p. 153.

9. Ibid.

10. Burchfield and Hancock, p. 11.

11. Bush, p. 162.

Chapter 6. Mr. Vice President

1. Mark Vittert, "Castro Won't Last a Year,'" *St. Louis Business Journal*, December 21, 1998, <http://stlouis .bcentral.com/stlouis/stories/1998/12/21/editorial2.html> (May 21, 2001).

2. Lou Cannon, *President Reagan: The Role of a Lifetime* (New York: Simon & Schuster, 1991), p. 123.

3. Randall Rothenberg, "In Search of George Bush," *The New York Times Magazine*, March 6, 1988, p. 48.

4. Paul F. Boller, Jr., *Presidential Campaigns* (New York: Oxford University Press, 1985), p. 373.

5. *The Class of the Twentieth Century* television program, episode: years 1976-1990, CEL Communications, Inc. and Arts and Entertainment Network, 1991.

Chapter 7. Campaign '88

1. Fitzhugh Green, *George Bush: An Intimate Portrait* (New York: Hippocrene Books, 1989), p. 217.

2. Public Broadcasting System, "Character Above All: Glossaries" transcript, <http://www.pbs.org/newshour/ character/glossaries/bush.html> (June 13, 2001).

3. Michael Riley, "Anatomy of a Disaster," *Time*, November 21, 1988, p. 38.

4. Bruce Curtis, "The Wimp Factor," *American Heritage*, November, 1989, p. 42.

5. George F. Will, "George Bush: The Sound of a Lapdog," *The Washington Post*, January 30, 1986, p. A25.

6. Michael R. Beschloss, "Character Above All" transcript, <http://www.pbs.org/newshour/character/ essays/bush.html> (March 14, 2001).

7. Personal interview with Brent Scowcroft, July 24, 2001.

8. Ibid.

9. Ibid.

10. Jack E. White, "Bush's Most Valuable Player," *Time*, November 14, 1988, pp. 20–21.

11. Herbert S. Parmet, *George Bush: The Life of a Lone Star Yankee* (New Brunswick, N.J.: Transaction Publishers, 2001), p. 336.

12. Personal interview with Michael Dukakis, June 29, 2001.

13. Ibid.

14. Ibid.

15. Ibid.

16. Ibid.

17. Mark J. Rozell, *The Press and the Bush Presidency* (Westport, Conn.: Praeger Publishers, 1996), p. 17.

18. Personal interview with Brent Scowcroft.

Chapter 8. Farewell to the Dictators

1. Herbert S. Parmet, *George Bush: The Life of a Lone Star Yankee* (New Brunswick, N.J.: Transaction Publishers, 2001), p. 375.

2. George Bush, *All The Best: My Life in Letters and Other Writings* (New York: A Lisa Drew Book, Charles Scribner's Sons, 1999), p. 432.

3. Personal interview with Marlin Fitzwater, June 11, 2001.

4. George Bush and Brent Scowcroft, *A World Transformed* (New York: Alfred A. Knopf, 1998), p. 148.

5. Parmet, p. 403.

6. Bush and Scowcroft, p. 149.

7. Michael R. Beschloss and Strobe Talbott, *At the Highest Levels: The Inside Story of the End of the Cold War* (Boston: Little, Brown and Company, 1993), p. 164.

8. George Bush, *All The Best: My Life in Letters and Other Writings*, p. 450.

9. Ibid.

10. Colin Powell with Joseph E. Persico, *My American Journey* (New York: Random House, 1995), p. 431, and Parmet, p. 418.

11. Ibid., p. 434.

12. Personal interview with Brent Scowcroft, July 24, 2001.

13. Ibid.

14. Personal interview with Marlin Fitzwater.

15. Personal interview with Brent Scowcroft.

Chapter 9. Promises, Promises

1. Barbara Bush, *Barbara Bush: A Memoir* (New York: A Lisa Drew Book, Charles Scribner's Sons, 1994), p. 337.

2. Lisa Zeff, executive producer, *Biography*, "Barbara Bush: First Mom," ABC, Inc. and A&E Networks, May 2001.

3. "Remarks at the Point of Light Award Presentation Ceremony for the Henderson Hall/Barcroft Elementary School Adopt-A-School Program in Arlington, Virginia." Bush Library presidential papers, March 11, 1991, <http://bushlibrary.tamu.edu/papers/1991/91031103.html> (June 26, 2001).

4. "Message to the House of Representatives Returning Without Approval the Family and Medical Leave Act," Bush Library presidential papers, June 29, 1990, <http://bushlibrary.tamu.edu/papers/1990/90062903.html> (June 22, 2001).

5. "The President's News Conference," Bush Library presidential papers, June 29, 1990, <http://bushlibrary.tamu.edu/papers/1990/90062900.html> (June 22, 2001).

6. Mark J. Rozell, *The Press and the Bush Presidency* (Westport, Conn.: Praeger Publishers, 1996), p. 73.

7. Personal interview with Marlin Fitzwater, June 11, 2001.

8. Personal interview with Michael Dukakis, June 29, 2001.

9. Personal interview with Brent Scowcroft, July 24, 2001.

10. Personal interview with Marlin Fitzwater.

11. "Statement on Signing the Americans with Disabilities Act of 1990," Bush Library presidential papers, July 26, 1990, <http://bushlibrary.tamu.edu./papers/1990/90072601.html> (June 22, 2001).

12. Personal interview with Marlin Fitzwater.

13. "Remarks on Signing the Bill Amending the Clean Air Act," Bush Library presidential papers, November 15, 1990, <http://bushlibrary.tamu.edu/papers/1990/90111501.html> (June 22, 2001).

14. Ibid.

15. Herbert S. Parmet, *George Bush: The Life of a Lone Star Yankee* (New Brunswick, N.J.: Transaction Publishers, 2001), p. 485.

16. "White House Fact Sheet on The Strategic Arms Reduction Treaty (START)," Bush Library presidential papers, July 31,1991, <http://bushlibrary.tamu.edu/papers/1991/91073108.html> (June 22, 2001).

17. Personal interview with Marlin Fitzwater.

18. George Bush, *All The Best: My Life in Letters and Other Writings* (New York: A Lisa Drew Book, Charles Scribner's Sons, 1999), p. 538

Chapter 10. "Not the Position I Would Have Preferred"

1. Michael Duffy, "Deficits Don't Matter; Votes Sure Do," *Time*, February 10, 1992, p. 25.

2. Mark J. Rozell, *The Press and the Bush Presidency* (Westport, Conn.: Praeger Publishers, 1996), p. 120.

3. "Earth Summit: Historic First Step," *Environmental Defense online newsletter*, October 1992 <http://www.environmentaldefense.org/pubs/edfletter/1992/Oct/a_summit.html> (June 26, 2001).

4. Ibid.

5. Barbara Bush, *Barbara Bush: A Memoir* (New York: A Lisa Drew Book, Charles Scribner's Sons, 1994), p. 464.

6. "The President's News Conference in Rio de Janeiro," Bush Library presidential papers, June 13, 1992, <http://bushlibrary.tamu.edu/papers/1992/92061300.html> (June 26, 2001),

7. Personal interview with Marlin Fitzwater, June 11, 2001.

8. Rozell, p. 127.

9. Transcript. "The First Clinton-Bush-Perot Presidential Debate, October 11, 1992, <http://www.debates.org/pages/trans92a1.html> (June 28, 2001).

10. Ibid.

11. Personal interview with Michael Dukakis, June 29, 2001.

12. Herbert S. Parmet, *George Bush: The Life of a Lone Star Yankee* (New Brunswick, N.J.: Transaction Publishers, 2001), p. 507.

13. George Bush, *All The Best: My Life in Letters and Other Writings* (New York: A Lisa Drew Book, Charles Scribner's Sons, 1999), p. 571.

14. Personal interview with Marlin Fitzwater.

15. Ibid.

16. Personal interview with Michael Dukakis.

17. Personal interview with Brent Scowcroft, July 24, 2001.

18. "Radio Address to the Nation on the Results of the Presidential Election," Bush Library presidential papers, November 7, 1992, <http://bushlibrary.tamu.edu/papers/1992/92110700.html> (June 22, 2001).

19. Barbara Bush, p. 508.

20. Stuart Eskenazi, "Luminaries celebrate Bush, christen his library," *Austin American-Statesman*, November 7, 1997, p. A1.

21. Ibid.

22. Kathy Lewis, "Thousands gather to dedicate Bush library:" "What they said" sidebar, *The Dallas Morning News*, p. 30A.

23. Eskenazi, p. A1.

Chapter 11. Legacy

1. William J. Ridings, Jr., and Stuart B. McIver, *Rating the Presidents: A Ranking of United States Leaders, From the Great and Honorable to the Dishonest and Incompetent* (New York: A Citadel Press Book, 2000), p. 268.

2. Ibid., p. 273.

3. "Historians Rank Presidential Leadership in New C-SPAN Survey," *American Presidents: Life Portraits*, February 21, 2000, <www.americanpresidents.org/survey/amp022100.asp> (July 25, 2001).

4. "C-SPAN Survey of Presidential Leadership: George Bush: Historian Survey Results," *American Presidents: Life Portraits, 2000*, <www.americanpresidents.org/survey/historians/40.asp> (July 25, 2001).

5. Roger J. Spiller, "A War Against History," *American Heritage*, February/March 2001, pp. 86–87.

6. Personal interview with Brent Scowcroft, July 24, 2001.

7. Ibid.

8. Ibid.

9. Personal interview with Marlin Fitzwater, June 11, 2001.

10. Ibid.

11. Personal interview with Michael Dukakis, June 29, 2001.

12. "Faces of the ADA," Americans with Disabilities Act Web site, <www.usdoj.gov/crt/ada/fmartin.htm> (June 22, 2001).

13. Personal interview with Michael Dukakis.

Further Reading

Bush, Barbara. *Barbara Bush: A Memoir*. New York: A Lisa Drew Book, Charles Scribner's Sons, 1994.

Bush, George. *All the Best: My Life in Letters and Other Writings*. New York: A Lisa Drew Book, Charles Scribner's Sons, 1999.

Francis, Sandra. *George Bush: Our Forty-First President*. Chanhassen, Minn.: The Child's World, 2002.

Judson, Karen. *Ronald Reagan*. Springfield, N.J.: Enslow Publishers, 1997.

King, John. *The Gulf War*. New York: Dillon Press, 1991.

Lands and Peoples: Crisis in the Middle East. Danbury, Conn.: Grolier, Inc., 1992.

Pelta, Kathy. *Texas*. Minneapolis: Lerner Publications Company, 1994.

Woog, Adam. *The United Nations*. San Diego: Lucent Books, 1993.

Internet Addresses

George Bush Presidential Library and Museum
http://bushlibrary.tamu.edu

The Presidential Museum in Odessa, Texas
http://www.presidentialmuseum.org

The White House
http://www.whitehouse.gov

Places to Visit

California

Ronald Reagan Presidential Library and Museum, Simi Valley. (800) 410–8354, (805) 522–8444. Ronald Reagan's presidential museum has exhibits relating to Vice President Bush and the Iran-Contra scandal, and includes a full scale reproduction of the White House Oval Office. Open year-round.

Connecticut

Museum of American Political Life, West Hartford. (860) 768–4090. The history of every United States presidential campaign is told through buttons, banners, photos, posted commentaries, and videotape. Open year-round.

Indiana

Dan Quayle Center and Museum, Huntington. (219) 356–6356. This is the only museum devoted exclusively to United States vice presidents. Included are artifacts about Quayle and all American vice presidents, and gifts given to Quayle by world leaders. Open year-round.

New York

United Nations Headquarters, New York City. (212) 963–8687. Guided tours lasting roughly forty-five minutes take visitors through the most important rooms. Also seen are sculptures and other works of art. Open year-round.

Texas

George Bush Presidential Library and Museum, College Station. (979) 260–9552. George Bush's presidential museum tells the forty-first president's life story, from his boyhood to his post-presidential years. It is the only presidential museum to include replicas of Air Force One, the president's official airplane, and Camp David, the president's private retreat in the mountains of Maryland. Open year-round.

The Petroleum Museum, Midland. (915) 683–4403. Antique oil rigs, dioramas, art, and a recreated main street from a typical 1920s oil boomtown tell the story of the oil industry in Texas. Open year-round.

The Presidential Museum, Odessa. (915) 332–7123. Campaign mementoes, medals, and a collection of the first ladies' gowns in miniature offer a look at the American presidency. Open year-round.

Washington, D.C.

The White House (202) 456–7041. Several rooms are open to visitors on certain weekday mornings. You can get tickets when you arrive or in advance through your senator or congressperson. Open year-round.

Index

A

Americans with Disabilities Act
of 1990, 85, 104, 105–106

B

Bentsen, Lloyd, 46, 64–65
Berlin Wall, 42, 73–74
Buchanan, Pat, 93, 94
Bush, Barbara Pierce, 17,
20–21, 23, 34, 36, 38,
49, 51, 69, 81–82
Bush, George Herbert Walker
childhood, 9–18
domestic policy, 71–73,
83–87, 88–89, 104–106
early political involvement,
36, 39, 41–43
engagement and marriage,
23, 26–27
oil industry, 31–40, 44
vice president, 53–62
World War II, 19–28
Bush, George Walker, 29, 101
Bush, John Ellis (Jeb), 36, 101
Bush, Pauline Robinson, 35, 36
Bush, Prescott, Sr., 9, 11, 13,
31, 36, 38, 46, 48, 95
Bush-Overbey Oil Development
Company, Inc., 35, 37

C

Carter, Jimmy, 51, 53, 54, 57,
59, 100
Central Intelligence Agency
(CIA), 51
Clean Air Act of 1970, 86, 104
Clinton, Bill, 9, 94–97, 99, 100,
104, 106

D

Dresser Industries, 31, 33, 35
Dukakis, Michael, 64–69, 84,
94, 95, 96, 105, 106

E

Eisenhower, Dwight D., 36, 38,
39, 101

F

Family and Medical Leave Act
of 1990, 83
Fitzwater, Marlin, 67, 72, 79,
84, 85, 88, 96, 104, 106
Ford, Gerald, 49, 51, 55, 57, 100
Ford, Guillermo (Billy), 76, 80

G

Gorbachev, Mikhail, 63, 74–75,
82, 87, 88, 90, 104

H

Hill, Anita, 88–89
Horton, Willie, 66–68
Hussein, Saddam, 6, 7, 102

I

Iran, 54, 55, 57, 60
Iran-Contra scandal, 61, 62,
    64, 65, 68, 86, 96, 99
Iraq, 5–8, 86
Iron Curtain countries, fall of,
    73, 75, 78, 87–88, 89–90,
    91, 103–104

J

John Birch Society, 43

K

Kuwait, 5–8, 86

L

Liedtke, Hugh, 37, 39, 40
Liedtke, William, 37, 39, 40

M

McCarthy, Joseph, 38, 95
McFarlane, Robert, 60, 61
Mitchell, George, 74, 85
Mondale, Walter, 57, 60

N

Nixon, Richard, 46–50
Noriega, Manuel, 75–80

O

Operation Desert Storm, *See*
    Persian Gulf War
Operation Just Cause, 76, 79
Operation Restore Hope, 98
Overbey, John, 35, 39

P

Panama, 75–80
People's Republic of China, 47,
    49, 51
Perot, H. Ross, 95, 96
Persian Gulf War, 5–8, 86, 97,
    102, 103, 104, 106
Points of Light Foundation, 83

Powell, Colin, 8

Q

Quayle, Dan, 64, 69

R

Reagan, Ronald, 9, 55–56, 57,
    59–61, 63, 65–67, 71, 104

S

Scowcroft, Brent, 66, 69, 79,
    80, 84, 87, 97, 102,
    103, 106
Souter, David, 85, 88
Soviet Union, 37, 38, 63, 73,
    87–91, 103
Strategic Arms Reduction
    Treaty (START), 87
Strategic Arms Reduction
    Treaty (START II), 98

T

Thomas, Clarence, 88–89

U

United Nations, 5, 47, 48, 79

V

Vietnam War, 44, 45, 94

W

Watergate scandal, 48, 49, 51
Weinberger, Caspar, 61, 96, 99
World War II, 17, 19–29, 37,
    97, 99

Y

Yale University, 29–32
Yarborough, Ralph, 43, 46
Yeltsin, Boris, 87, 89, 98

Z

Zapata Petroleum 37, 39,
    40, 44